access to philosophy

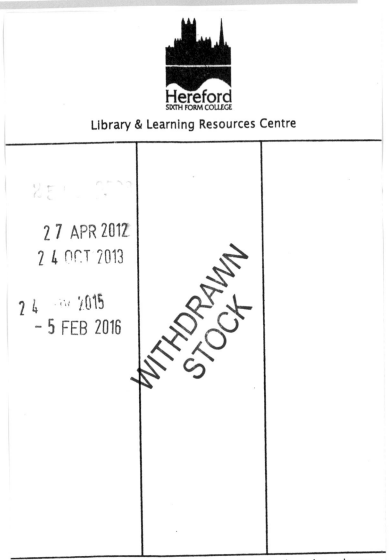

Hereford
SIXTH FORM COLLEGE

Library & Learning Resources Centre

This book is to be returned on or before the last date shown.

access to philosophy

ETHICAL THEORY

Second Edition

Mel Thompson

Hodder Murray

A MEMBER OF THE HODDER HEADLINE GROUP

The publishers would like to thank the following for permission to reproduce material:
Bettmann/CORBIS for the photos on pages 94 and 104.
For text acknowledgements see page 164.

Although every effort has been made to ensure that website addresses are correct at time of going to press, Hodder Murray cannot be held responsible for the content of any website mentioned in this book. It is sometimes possible to find a relocated web page by typing in the address of the home page for a website in the URL window of your browser.

Orders: please contact Bookpoint Ltd, 130 Milton Park, Abingdon, Oxon OX14 4SB. Telephone: (44) 01235 827720. Fax: (44) 01235 400454. Lines are open from 9.00 to 6.00, Monday to Saturday, with a 24-hour answering service. Visit our website at www.hoddereducation.co.uk.

© Mel Thompson 2005
First published in 1999 by Hodder Murray, a member of the Hodder Headline Group
338 Euston Road
London NW1 3BH

This edition 2005

Impression number 10 9 8 7 6 5 4 3 2
Year   2010 2009 2008 2007 2006

Cover photo courtesy of Kevin Kelley/Getty Images.
Typeset in New Baskerville 9 point by Transet Limited, Coventry, England.
Printed in Malta.

A catalogue record for this title is available from the British Library.

ISBN-10: 0 340 88344 8
ISBN-13: 987-0-340-88344 0

Contents

Preface to the 2nd Edition

Access books are written mainly for students studying for examinations, particularly GCSE, Advanced Subsidiary (AS) Level and Advanced (A2) Level. A number of features have therefore been included to assist students: each chapter opens with brief definitions of useful terms and ends with a summary of the main points, along with some examination-type questions.

For this second edition, the original text has been retained as far as possible for many of the sections, with only minor additions or corrections. It is hoped that this will allow the new and old editions to be used alongside one another without difficulty. However, to address the needs of students that have become apparent since publication of the first edition, some sections have been strengthened and new material has been added. In particular, you will find that:

- the section on freedom and determinism in Chapter 3 has been augmented and clarified;
- further material has been added to Chapter 10, on Kant;
- the chapter on Religious Ethics has been enlarged, with an outline of the principles and the authority upon which the ethics of each religion is based, and a brief account of the Divine Command theory of ethics;
- the chapter on Conscience has been augmented;
- a new chapter has been added, giving an outline of modern Virtue Ethics.

As with other books in the *Access* series, *Ethical Theory* is designed to give an overview of the subject and to act as a springboard for further reading and study. Additional study material, suitable for this level, is listed in the 'Further Reading' section.

Feedback from both students and teachers is welcome. Please contact me on **www.mel-thompson.co.uk**, where you will also find information on my other publications and additional notes suitable for students at A-Level.

Mel Thompson
June 2004

1 Introduction

KEYWORDS

descriptive ethics – descriptions of human moral behaviour

normative ethics – arguments about right and wrong

deontological – to do with duty

axiological – to do with values

meta-ethics – the examination of the nature of ethical statements

applied ethics – the application of ethical theory to specific issues

Ethics is the study of right and wrong; of the moral choices people make and the way in which they seek to justify them. Ethics is an enormous subject. There is almost no aspect of life that does not in some way inform the process of moral decision making, and equally, there is almost no aspect of life to which ethics cannot be applied.

1 Four basic approaches

In order to make the subject more manageable, we need to start by mapping out different areas of ethics. There are four basic approaches:

a) Descriptive ethics

Descriptive ethics examines the moral choices and values that are held in a particular society. So, for example, one might say that certain societies allow polygamy and others do not, or that some impose the death sentence for certain crimes. Not only can you describe what people do, you can also give an objective description of the reasons they give for doing it. Descriptive ethics of this kind are part sociology and also part moral psychology. But the key feature of all descriptive ethics is that it does not examine or question issues of right or wrong. It simply states what is the case.

Now, there is a place for descriptive ethics, because without information about situations and how people respond to them, there would be little material upon which the other forms of ethics could go to work. But in itself, descriptive ethics is limited, and a student who tried to answer an ethical question simply by describing situations would not be considered to have got to grips with the subject. It is the fact of the variety of such behaviour and the experience of being free to choose to go along with what others are doing or take a different option, that leads to issues of right and wrong.

b) Normative ethics

Normative ethics examines the norms by which people make moral choices. It involves questions about one's *duty* (what one 'ought' to do, often termed **deontological questions**) and questions about the *values* that are expressed through moral choices (what constitutes a 'good' life, sometimes termed **axiological questions**). Normative ethics takes the step that descriptive ethics avoids. It looks at a statement about behaviour and asks 'Is it right to do that?' So, for example, in descriptive ethics you simply point out the number of abortions that take place. In normative ethics you go on to ask 'But is it *right* to have an abortion?' In other words, you are asking about the norms of behaviour – the bases upon which people decide right from wrong.

c) Meta-ethics

Ethical theory includes discussion of what moral language is all about and how it can be justified. Such discussion is sometimes described as **meta-ethics**. During much of the 20th century there was a general tendency in Britain and the United States for philosophers to concentrate on language. In other words, instead of simply asking 'Is it right?' they tended to ask 'What does it mean to say that something is right?' or 'What am I doing when I make that sort of statement?' This was in response to a line of thinking that said that all moral propositions were in fact meaningless. Meta-ethics represented the attempt to find out what people did mean – since, clearly, those who argued that things were right or wrong thought that what they said definitely *did* have meaning!

d) Applied ethics

The most important and immediate aspect of ethics however is **applied ethics**. There would be no interest in ethics at all unless there were issues where genuine moral choices and values were expressed and questioned. Some of the most important areas of applied ethics today concern the ethics of life and death, medical ethics, the ethics of sexuality and relationships, feminist ethics, bioethics (particularly issues concerning genetics), legal ethics, environmental ethics, business ethics and particularly the issues of peace, war and terrorism.

Books on applied ethics examine the choices that are made in these spheres in the light of ethical theories. Ethical theory and applied ethics need to be examined alongside one another. You can test out a theory by applying it to practical situations and see if it yields reasonable results, or you can reflect on common-sense decisions made in particular situations and ask what ethical theories are presupposed by them.

2 An historical perspective

Ethical theory is a branch of philosophy and, as such, has been influenced by the general questions about life and its meaning that have been asked by philosophers over the centuries. It has also been shaped by the social, political and religious culture within which it has developed. To get something of an overview of ethics, let us look at some key features in the history of ethical theory within Western thought:

- In ancient Greece, particularly in the writings of Plato and Aristotle, you have debates about what makes for the good life, about the ideal qualities a person should have and about the relationship between virtue and the quest for happiness.
- With the Natural Law approach of Aquinas you have a medieval attempt to bring together Aristotle's idea that everything should fulfil its natural end or purpose, with the Christian doctrine that all things are created by God, in order to provide a comprehensive view of what can be considered natural and right.
- Later we find four different approaches: Hobbes thought ethics should be based on a contractual agreement between people; Hume thought it should be based on sentiment rather than reason, since people were able to have a natural sympathy for others; the utilitarians thought it should be based on the expected results of action; and Kant thought that ethical principles could be based on pure practical reason alone.
- Some nineteenth- and twentieth-century thinkers (e.g. Nietzsche and Sartre) have considered ethics in the light of the self-development of individuals, or the personal questions people ask about life and its meaning. They argued that ethics is not something to be discovered, but created and shaped by our own choices.
- For much of the twentieth century ethical theory was dominated by arguments about whether ethical language was meaningless. For some thinkers, ethics was seen as a covert way of expressing one's own preferences or giving commands.
- In the last three decades of the twentieth century there was a revival of interest in applied ethics, and also in theories of contract and virtue, and a re-examination of many earlier ethical arguments.

3 The challenge of ethics

In its broadest context, ethics is the study of human conduct. Questions about what a person 'ought' to do therefore lead to more fundamental questions about the nature and purpose of human life. But equally, views about life, whether they arise within philosophy or religion, will have an impact on human conduct, and therefore on ethics.

Ethics is not simply concerned with average standards of behaviour. Rather, it is about the quest to find what is right and good and the best way to live. Of course, that is not to take a narrow moral view, in the sense of condemning all who disagree with a particular code, but to emphasise that we want to find a basis of value by which to live, on the assumption that justice and happiness will follow.

In doing this, of course, we often have to concentrate on what is worst in human nature. It is in contemplating acts of cruelty that we most easily start to perceive what is essential about kindness, in acts of selfishness that we intuit what it would be to act selflessly.

One of the questions with which every student of ethics has to struggle is whether ethics can be considered 'objective':

- Can moral questions be decided on the basis of facts, or do they always depend on values and opinions?
- Is there any such thing as goodness, over and above the label 'good' that we give those things of which we approve?
- What would convince me that a statement about human rights or wrongs is final or absolute?
- Is everything simply a matter of personal choice and taste?

There was a time – about the mid 1960s – when it could reasonably be assumed that any quest for an objective definition of 'goodness' or 'virtue' was doomed. Many philosophers considered that moral language merely expressed the desires, intentions or preferences of individuals, and posed few challenges.

Now, in the early years of the 21st century, however, ethics has been transformed and dominated by applied ethics. The world set an agenda and expected ethics to come up with some guidelines. From international terrorism to genetic engineering, key issues demanded serious moral consideration.

Ethical positions are not always made explicit, and are often confused. Pick up any newspaper and you will find a mixture of facts, values and arguments – along with a fair measure of fantasy and speculation, depending on which paper you choose! The challenge of ethics is to cut through the resulting confusion, to distinguish between facts, values and arguments, to clarify the grounds upon which comments are being made, to examine the beliefs and emotions that are expressed, and to see whether the arguments are logically sound.

2 Ethical Arguments

KEYWORDS

non-cognitive – describes a statement that gives no factual information

relativist – the view that there are no universal moral norms

absolutist – the view that it is possible to establish universal moral norms

This chapter sets out what you need in order to present a sound ethical argument, the three basic approaches taken to ethics, the issue of how you relate particular situations to general ethical principles, and the social context of ethics in terms of rights and responsibilities.

1 Presenting an ethical argument

You need to be aware of three distinct elements in any good ethical argument: facts, values and the logic of the argument itself. So:

(a) You should know the facts about the situation you are considering:

● You should find out what the law says about this situation.
● If you, the presenter of the argument, or the person whose moral dilemma you are describing, is religious, you will want to know what the relevant religion has to say about it.
● You should try to understand exactly what is happening, the motives of those concerned and the predicted outcome of what is being done (that is, if any outcome can be predicted).
● You also need to know if there are any particular circumstances that make this situation unique. (Of course, you could argue that every situation is unique – after all, no two people are the same. But this means something rather more than that, for there are some situations where someone is in such a special set of circumstances that the normal rules of behaviour no longer seem to apply. So, for example, there are things you might do if your life depended on it that you would not choose to do otherwise.)

(b) You should consider carefully the norms and values by which that situation is to be evaluated:

● If you are arguing that something is right or wrong, you must be clear about the grounds upon which you are making that claim, and the values that are implied by it. If you are not, then you may fail to appreciate why someone else, faced with the same facts, comes to quite a different conclusion about the rights and wrongs of the matter. What may seem a trivial matter to one person may be important to another.

(c) You should be aware of the nature of the claim you are making, and of any possible challenge that could be made to that claim:

● In other words, it could be that someone wants to argue that all moral claims are really no more than expressing a personal preference (I say it is right because that is what I want to see happen). If you want to argue against this, you should think carefully about the logical basis upon which you can do so. If you don't, then you too will be accused of doing no more than expressing a personal preference, and the argument will have failed.

Like most philosophical arguments, ethical claims move from *premises* to *conclusions*. The premises will include both the facts of the situation and also the norms of behaviour used by yourself or those involved. The conclusion may be challenged on two grounds:

● That you did not argue logically from the premises to the conclusion. In other words, even given those circumstances, and given those moral values, it does not follow that this or that action is therefore wrong. There might be another way of seeing the whole situation.
● More likely, however, is the challenge that you are wrong about the premises. Thus someone will say, 'I disagree with you because I don't think (for example) that you have to preserve human life at all costs, because I feel that the quality of life …', etc. Here the debate is about norms. Equally, however, there could be a straight disagreement about the facts. So, for example, in a court of law there may be considerable debate about whether a person committed some act while the balance of his or her mind was disturbed. If disturbed, that constitutes an important premise to take into account, and the person will not be blamed in the same way as a person who did the same thing while fully aware of his or her actions.

2 Three basic views

When it comes to moral language and ethical theories there are three widely held basic views:

a) Non-cognitive

It may be argued that moral language is not really saying anything objective, but is simply a covert way of expressing one's feelings or recommending a course of action. Such approaches are termed **non-cognitive**, since they do not allow that ethical language gives knowledge of anything other than the feelings and preferences of the person using it. In effect: if I like something, I call it 'good', if I dislike it, I call it 'bad', and there's an end to the matter.

On that basis, there is really nothing to discuss. We are not talking about values or principles. We are not seeking any objective way of saying whether something is right or wrong; we are simply talking about personal wishes.

b) Relativist

A **relativist** approach says, in effect, that no two situations are exactly the same. A person's choices will be related to a unique set of circumstances, and it makes no sense to generalise or try to say that one view is always right and another always wrong. There are no universal moral rules; each person should decide what is right according to his or her particular circumstances.

c) Absolutist

Finally, there is the attempt to find a framework of ideas that enables us to argue that some things are always right and others always wrong. This is sometimes referred to as an **absolutist** approach, but this does not mean that it claims that there are fixed moral rules (although, of course, some people will argue just that), but that moral decisions are related to principles that can be applied universally.

Naturally enough, a book on ethical theory is going to be concerned particularly with the grounds on which people have taken this third approach. Within it you have some arguments to the effect that there are absolute moral principles that can be known by pure reason (**rationalist ethics**) or are commanded by God, others that examine virtues and the qualities that make for the good life and what moral positions will promote them (**virtue ethics**), a third group that looks at the results of an action and weighs up whether it is good or bad on that basis (**consequentialist ethics**, including **utilitarianism**), and a fourth will ask whether something conforms to a rational interpretation of its natural end or purpose (**Natural Law**). Others approach ethics from the standpoint of the implied contract that exists between people who live together in a society, part of which may be expressed in terms of laws, and part in terms of the rights and responsibilities that can be expected of members of that society.

3 Theory and practice

KEY ISSUE   Relating individual situations to general moral principles.

This book is specifically about ethical theory. In other words, it looks at the claims that are made about right and wrong, the arguments used and the meaning of ethical language.

In the course of the book, we shall be looking at a whole variety of situations. We could not study ethics without doing so, except in the most abstract and dry way. But those who are looking at this book as preparation for an examination course in ethics should be aware that the examples given here are only brought in to illustrate how the theory works. When it comes to examination questions, it will be necessary to have a good working knowledge of the actual situations in which people make moral choices. In other words, if you are looking at medical ethics, it is important to know what the law has to say and what medical options are possible in the situation you are considering. Ethics is not limited to facts, but it is based on them. An ethical argument without a factual base is unsatisfactory, because moral decisions are always made in particular situations and under the influence of a number of different factors; leave them out of account and you are hardly going to understand the real moral dilemma involved.

For this reason, there is a range of books in this *Access to Philosophy* series that give information on particular moral issues such as life and death, sexuality and family relations or the environment. Once you start to work on particular ethical issues you may need to use them, or similar books, in order to appreciate the context within which the various ethical theories may be evaluated. In addition to books on applied ethics, daily newspapers are a valuable resource, for they describe a wide range of issues, many of which attract comments about what is right or wrong with little thought as to the norms of conduct that such comments imply, nor to the logic by which the conclusions may be drawn from such norms.

a) General arguments and particular situations

When you start to examine the moral choices that people make, you can become bogged down in the variety of particular situations. Some of these present clear-cut choices, and the dilemmas involved are straightforward, even if the act of choosing what to do is difficult because the choices are almost equally attractive or disagreeable. In other situations, additional factors come into play and matters are not so easily resolved. *In fact, no two situations are identical, and it is therefore difficult to frame a rule by which all possible situations can be assessed fairly.*

To do ethics, one therefore needs to stand back from the many particular situations and seek the underlying principles that should govern action. But why use 'should' here? By what right does any one person say what another 'should' do? You may adopt a set of rules for yourself, but is it fair to impose them on others?

Let us therefore take this step by step:

- You start with particular situations – they present a variety of choices and responses.
- You then examine the rules that people actually apply to the process of deciding what is the right thing to do.
- You compare such rules with those that you yourself would choose to adopt, and assess to what extent any differences between your rules and those that seem to be applied by others are due to different circumstances, or fundamentally different ideas of what constitutes right and wrong.
- You then examine the norms, values and ideas that are expressed through those rules.

Looking at what people actually do in various situations, and also at the sort of language they use to justify what they do, leads inevitably to questions about the basis of any such justification. So, by asking what is right or wrong and how people should act, you are really asking about the grounds upon which something may be considered right or wrong. In other words, you are asking about *the norms of human behaviour.*

Example
Let us take an entirely hypothetical situation. The President of the United States is accused of having a sexual relationship with a woman other than his wife. He first denies this publicly, but is eventually forced by weight of evidence to admit that he acted inappropriately, but questions whether what he did should count as 'having sexual relations'.

There are various arguments to be considered and positions that may be taken:

- Sexual activity between consenting adults should remain a private matter, and should not become the subject of public debate or censure.
- All those who hold high office should accept the moral norms of the society they represent.
- The sex may remain a private matter, but the President should not have lied about it, since truthfulness and integrity are required of someone holding his office.
- Personal matters are irrelevant as long as it does not interfere with a person's job. If the President is still functioning well as President, what does it matter?

- Other Presidents in the past have had affairs, so why should this be any different?

As you unpack these and other responses, some fundamental ethical issues emerge:

- The right to individual privacy.
- The moral status of extra-marital sex.
- The value of honesty.

And beneath these there are more general questions about:

- The function of those who hold positions of public responsibility. By accepting such positions, do they thereby set aside their normal right to privacy in all matters that might affect their public role?
- The position of marriage and the family in society.
- The value of absolute honesty as opposed to political expediency.

At this level, although initiated by a discussion of a particular situation – one that involves a person in a unique position in society – the ethical debate has shifted onto the norms by which that action is judged. Once that happens, it is largely irrelevant to give a list of former Presidents who have acted similarly, for when it comes to normative ethics, the fact that other people do the same does not make it either right or wrong. At best, the historical parallels are a matter for 'descriptive' ethics.

This example illustrates what we will be concerned with in this book:

- We shall need to look at what makes morality possible. Are we free to choose what to do? Should we be blamed for things over which we had no control? When is 'I couldn't help it' a valid excuse?
- But once we are satisfied about situations where a free choice is made, we have to ask whether there are any absolute rules that can be applied, or whether all situations have to be judged individually.
- Then there comes the fundamental question about whether there are basic principles that should underpin all morality, principles that arise because we are human beings, and that can be applied to all of us. Or should moral choices be made on the basis of the expected results of an action? Do we, in other words, act for a purpose, and therefore judge all action to be right or wrong to the extent that it fulfils or fails to fulfil that purpose?
- We shall then need to ask about the way in which the values that apply to moral choices, and which are therefore used to underpin ethical debate, relate to other fundamental values that people hold. In particular, how these relate to ideas about the purpose of life that are expressed through religion.
- Finally, we shall have to face various challenges to morality from those who might claim that neither religion nor morality has any factual basis, and that it is all either voluntarily accepted illusion, or else imposed for

reasons of social or political control. In other words, when we try to act morally, we shall have to ask whether we are just conning ourselves, or whether we are being conned by our upbringing and conditioning.

b) Every act is global in its implications

Whatever approach you take to ethics – whether based on absolute rules or on the expected results of an action – the implications of moral choice spread outwards until eventually they become global. The issues raised become such that they can be applied in different ways to all situations. It is this flowing to and fro among the individual, the society of which he or she is a part, and the nature of life as a whole, that makes ethics so fascinating – for nothing is ultimately insignificant; everything reflects a greater whole of which it is but a tiny part.

Ethical arguments do not exist on their own, but are based on beliefs and values that exist prior to the moral dilemma that is being considered – indeed, if there were no beliefs and values, the whole idea of moral choice would become meaningless, because there would be no basis for calling any action good or bad.

It works both ways: ethics is informed by fundamental beliefs and values. But also, fundamental beliefs and values may not be examined or appreciated until a moral choice is made that highlights them. Thus, if you want to know a person's values, look at their ethical choices.

4 Rights and responsibilities

KEY ISSUE   So far in this chapter, we have concentrated on the choices that individuals make and the criteria that they use to decide whether these are right or wrong. In other words, we have been looking at individuals and the theories that link their actions to some overall sense of value or purpose. But that is not the only way in which ethics can be approached. Most moral dilemmas arise within a social context; they are about the way people treat one another, and about their rights and responsibilities.

It is quite possible therefore to start with society, rather than with the individual, and look at individual actions in the light of what society needs. There has been a long tradition of this, as we shall see, from Plato's arguments about the right relationship between three different classes of people in the state, through Hobbes or Locke in looking at the contractual basis of social behaviour, to thinkers like Hegel and

Marx who see moral norms as arising out of a changing social and political situation. Here ethics overlaps with social and political theories, but its specific contribution lies in an examination of the rights that individuals are deemed to have as members of a society and the responsibilities that such membership entails.

Of course, considering society and its rules raises another problem for ethics. For a person may do what is considered 'right', not out of conviction or conscious choice, but because it is what society expects and as a result of social training. Is such an action genuinely moral? Does its moral validity depend on the individual who performs it, or the society that has developed and inculcated that social norm?

And here we are back to the question of relativism, for we noted above that different societies have different ethical norms. What is accepted as good and right in one society is outlawed in another. There is therefore yet another layer of argument to be added – a layer that considers the rights and responsibilities that actually exist within a society and asks if they can be justified rationally. In other words, is there a deeper reasoning that can assess what society is and how it is formed? This was indeed the concern of thinkers like Plato, Hobbes, Locke and, in modern times, Rawls. *Ethics is concerned with a sense of justice and the way in which it may be embodied in the contracts – written or otherwise – that bind people together in a social or political unit.*

Summary List

- Ethical arguments need to distinguish between facts and values.
- There are three fundamental approaches within ethics: non-cognitive, relativist and absolutist.
- In practice, individual situations are generally examined in the light of the underlying moral principles. Equally, particular situations have implications for the framing of universal principles.
- Ethics may start either with situations of individual moral choice, or with the perceived needs of society as a whole.

Questions

1. What elements need to be included if you are to present a sound ethical argument? Which of them, if any, do you think should take priority? Give your reasons.

For this question, make sure you distinguish carefully between facts and values, both of which are needed, along with an idea of exactly what you are claiming – an absolute rule, an expression of a preference, etc. Whichever you choose to see as taking priority, the other two can be shown to relate to it.

2. 'Every situation is unique.' Do you agree with this statement? Does it invalidate any use of universal moral principles? How would you know the right thing to do in a situation that really is unique?

It is important to show that you appreciate the problems of applying absolute rules to a variety of particular situations. It is equally important to recognise that, however important the particular situation being considered, all moral language presupposes a shared understanding and shared meaning. It could be argued that, however unique a situation, we can only understand it in relationship to others.

General essay questions on the same two issues:

3. The presentation of facts alone does not constitute an ethical argument. Discuss.

4. Ethics requires a balance between particular situations and universal principles. Discuss.

Note:
Most questions on ethics either start with, or should be illustrated by, particular moral dilemmas. To present a sound ethical argument, you should be aware of the relevant facts, but also know how to evaluate them in the light of the various ethical theories, and the values that are implied in the moral choices to be made. In this book, however, we are dealing with ethical theory. The questions are therefore of a more general nature, although you should try to illustrate your answers with reference to one or more of the issues you are studying.

3 What Makes Morality Possible?

KEYWORDS

determinism – the view that all actions are explicable in terms of their causes, and are therefore inevitable

reductionism – the view that actions are no more than their underlying physical processes

compatibilism – the view that a measure of human freedom is compatible with an acceptance of the universal principle of cause and effect

naturalistic fallacy – trying to argue from an 'is' to an 'ought'

maxim – the moral principle governing an action

This chapter looks at what is required in order for an action to be considered morally significant.

1 Three basic requirements

Ethics is concerned with the norms of human behaviour, with the choices people make and the way in which they justify those choices. Therefore it would seem that there must be at least three essential requirements for an action to be considered morally significant:

- that it involves (directly or indirectly) one or more human beings;
- that it involves a situation in which rational thought could be applied to the implications of possible courses of action;
- that there is a sufficient degree of freedom involved to permit the possibility of alternative courses of action, and thus of the validity of choice.

Let us look briefly at each of these.

a) Human action

A machine that is incapable of thought cannot be blamed for what it does. Thus, although one may claim to 'hate' computers when, for example, some administrative error is blamed on the operation of a computer system, the computer itself is not to blame for any inconvenience caused. As a machine, it is dependent upon those who program it or use it. If something is wrong, one should blame the conscious agent, not the unconscious tool. Thus, a murderer cannot claim that it was the knife that entered his or her victim, and therefore that the knife was to blame for the subsequent death.

In other words, there needs to be a human agent if we are to apply moral arguments. Animals may hunt and kill one another, volcanoes may erupt and bring about terrible destruction, but none of this has to do with ethics, for no human agency is involved.

b) Rational thought

Generally speaking, unconscious agents do not count morally. That is simply because unconscious agents (like non-human agents) are not in a position to weigh up a situation and choose how to act.

Example
Suppose a person has a heart attack and dies at the wheel of a car, which subsequently veers out of control and kills someone. The person who has died is no longer able to control the car. The action of swerving off the road and killing the pedestrian is not one in which there is any conscious decision or obvious negligence. On the other hand, one might ask:

● Did the person driving the car know of any heart condition?
● Had he or she been warned by a doctor not to drive?

If the person had been warned, then he or she must have taken a decision to drive in spite of the dangers. That decision was free and conscious and contributed directly to the death of the pedestrian. The decision, rather than what happened after the heart attack, could therefore be considered morally wrong.

On the other hand, even if the decision to drive had been taken against medical advice, were there exceptional circumstances that justified the risk? For example, was the driver attempting to get a seriously ill person to hospital, being the only person around who could do so? If so, can the risk be justified in the light of the probabilities that could be foreseen at the time of the decision? Could it still be justified in this way, even in the light of the subsequent death? Whether justified or not, the moral issue concerns the rational choice, not the events that took place once the person was no longer able to act rationally. In this case, you might blame the driver for his or her decision to drive, rather than for the death of the pedestrian.

c) Freedom

If you are absolutely free to do whatever you choose, you can be held responsible for your actions. On the other hand, are you ever absolutely free? A common form of defence offered by someone who has been accused of something that is either illegal or deemed immoral is that he or she was not free to choose to do anything else.

You may, for example, find yourself acting as an agent, following the rules laid down by an individual or by society. In this case, you are conscious of what you are doing, but your actions are likely to be considered from a moral point of view only to the extent that you are deemed to be free to accept, reject or challenge the order you are given, or the function you are expected to perform in society. The anticipated consequences of rejecting or challenging that function is taken into consideration in assessing moral significance. Thus, for example, if you obey an order because someone is pointing a gun at your head, the fact that you will be killed if you disobey is a significant factor to be taken into account. Are you free in such circumstances?

In order to answer that question, we need to examine the nature of freedom in more detail.

2 Causes and conditioning

It is generally accepted that all things are brought about by causes that pre-exist them. If this were not so, anything could happen for no reason, and common sense as well as science would be utterly undermined. We may not actually understand why everything in the world is as it is, but we generally accept that (if we had enough relevant information) everything is theoretically capable of being understood.

Fundamental arguments about the nature of causation are beyond the scope of this book, but we should note that there are two ways to approach the matter:

● One can argue that if X is seen to follow Y on a number of occasions, and never occurs without Y first occurring, then we have evidence for a causal connection between X and Y. The more occasions we observe X following Y, the more likely that causal connection becomes. We can never achieve certainty this way, but only a very high degree of probability. This argument was put forward by David Hume; it is empirical (based on evidence) and it represents the 'inductive' approach of science. Hume thought that a 'chance' event was simply one about which we did not know all the causal factors: ''tis commonly allowed by philosophers that what the vulgar call chance is nothing but a secret and conceal'd cause' (from *A Treatise of Human Nature*).
● One can hold that the human mind works in such a way that it will always seek causes for each and every event. Even though we cannot find a cause at the moment, we assume that there must be one. This was the approach taken by Immanuel Kant; our minds impose the idea of causality upon our experience.

As far as ethics is concerned, the crucial question is this: *Are the causes of an event (either observed or assumed) such that they define the event absolutely?*

If they do, it follows that everything that will happen in the future is in theory predictable from causes that exist in the present. It is impossible, given the present reality, for the future to be other than absolutely determined. We may think that we are free to choose what to do, but such freedom is merely an illusion created by the very complex process that goes on in the human brain. We think we are choosing, whereas in fact we are running through a very complex calculation whose outcome is already determined.

This approach is called **determinism**, and it is important for the philosophy of science, where it is often argued that Newtonian physics is essentially deterministic. One aspect of a determinist approach, which is particularly important for the philosophy of mind, is called **reductionism**. A reductionist argues that what we think of as thoughts are in fact *no more than* electrical impulses in the brain. Our actions are merely movements occasioned by chemical and electrical activity. Everything is *reduced* to its simplest physical components. Clearly, if reductionism is correct, then it makes little sense to say that we are free to choose how to act.

a) Forms of determinism

- **Hard determinism** is as described above, namely that every event is determined by its pre-existing causes. This does not imply that we can know a single 'cause' of every 'effect', but that – taken as a whole – the network of causes and conditions that exist at any one moment are sufficient to determine everything that will happen in the future. A hard determinist would generally take the view that freedom is an illusion, and that we are not logically justified in claiming responsibility for our actions, even if we personally feel that we are free and responsible.

- **Soft determinism** is the view that, although events are subject to the influence of a large number of causes and conditions, they are not wholly determined by them. Hence there is scope for an individual to take responsibility for his or her choices, although recognising that the scope for choice is limited by physical, social or psychological factors. (For a soft determinist, whatever happens may be in line with the physical sequence of cause and effect, but *the mind can select from the almost infinite number of possible physical actions that can take place.* Thus, in replying to a question, my tongue is equally physically capable of articulating 'Yes' or 'No'. In terms of physical causation, at the moment when I reply, there is nothing to choose between the two words. Morally, and in terms of my experience, there is everything to choose between them.)

- One may also argue for **theological determinism**, which is the view (found in some branches of Christianity and in Islam) that God has already determined everything that will happen. In terms of philosophy, this position was taken by Leibniz, who held that everything was ultimately reducible to infinitely small parts, having no physical dimensions and therefore mental rather than physical, called *monads*. He believed that God had set up a 'pre-established harmony' such that, at the moment when I would decide to move my arm, for example, the arm would actually be moved by God. Hence, in spite of the experience of freedom and choice, actions were already fixed by God, and harmonised to fit in with my choices.

Note:

For those studying the philosophy of religion, it may be worth considering the traditional 'problem of evil' in this context. How can a loving, all-powerful and all-knowing God allow human freedom, knowing that such freedom brings with it the possibility of suffering and evil?

b) Conditioning

It would be foolish to claim that we are absolutely free, for we need to take into consideration the conditions that influence us and (if you want to use that term) 'determine' what we do. We are influenced by personal, religious, cultural, social and political factors that are all part of our 'conditioning'. Even if we do not consciously reflect upon them, we carry with us values and visions from our environment, either because we wish to continue them, or because we wish consciously to rebel against them. Either way, they influence us and even if any one of them cannot 'determine' an action, taken together they tend to reduce the scope for free choice.

The more a person becomes aware of his or her conditioning, the more it can be taken into account when evaluating moral choices. The awareness of those conditions that prevail at the time when a moral decision is made is crucial in appreciating its significance. We shall see later that relativism – the claim that there are no universal moral rules because everything depends on particular circumstances – is an important feature in ethical debate. Relativism is essentially about whether conditions, since they vary from place to place and time to time, make it impossible to set down universal moral rules.

But notice that conditioning suggests soft determinism, not hard; it does not say that a future event or choice is necessary, only that the freedom to choose is limited by conditions.

c) How does all this square with our experience of freedom?

One way out of this problem is not to start with the idea of cause and effect that we find in the world (or impose upon the world) but to start with the actual experience of moral choice. I experience myself as free, and it is that freedom with which I am concerned. It is a view put forward by Kant (see Chapter 10), who argued that we could be at one and the same time *phenomenally* determined (i.e. determined as far as we appear to the senses) and *noumenally* free (free as we are in ourselves).

This is important scientifically since, as our knowledge of human behaviour and particularly brain activity increases, it may be possible to predict the response to a situation with great accuracy, even if the subject thought he or she was free – which can lead us into the realm of determinism and reductionism.

It happens on a casual level as well: 'I just knew you'd do that!' and 'Typical!' are comments that come as a result of predicting what had, from a person's point of view, been experienced as free choices. They tend to irritate precisely because being a free agent is so deeply important to our sense of self, and the thought that we are totally predictable suggests that we are no more than automata.

There is one important point that needs to be established here before we can go on to make any sense of ethics: *Even if determinism and reductionism are true, they are irrelevant to the process of moral decision-making.*

This may sound odd since, if everything is determined, my choice is an illusion and I cannot be blamed for what I do. If determinism is true, ethics would seem to be irrelevant. But that is not in fact the case for, if determinism is true:

- the illusion of freedom is a necessary and determined feature of human experience;
- the experience of choice is necessary and determined;
- the whole argument about ethics is itself already determined.

In other words, we could not, since we are human beings with the brains and faculties we have, do other than get into discussion about ethical issues. And reductionists cannot help but argue that all our actions are reduced to brain activity, because their brain activity determines that they should do so. *If determinism is universally applied, it cannot support one side rather than another in any moral argument.* So, even if the claim that we are 100% determined is true, that does not stop us having moral dilemmas.

Ethics is concerned with the human level of operation. It is indeed true that there is electrical activity in my brain and chemical activity in my muscles corresponding to everything I think and do, but that does not imply that the things I think and do are *the same as* that electrical and chemical activity. It may be that brain activity is a necessary physical component of the process of thought (and the way in which drugs influence thought is an example of the direct link between brains and minds), but it does not follow (as the reductionist claims) that minds are 'nothing but' brain activity, any more than music is 'nothing but' sound waves in the air. Without sound waves, there is no music; but the meaning of 'music' transcends the sound waves that deliver it to our ears.

d) Some useful terms

It is important to be aware of the philosophical terms used for the range of possibilities in this freedom/determinism debate:

- **Libertarianism** is the view that determinism is false, that people are free to choose how to act and that they may therefore be held responsible for their actions.
- **Incompatibilism** is the view that determinism is true and is incompatible with the idea of human freedom and moral responsibility. This is also known as hard determinism.
- **Compatibilism** is the view that determinism may be true, and that events may be predictable, but that human beings still have some measure of choice about how they act. In other words, a degree of freedom is logically compatible with determinism. This is also known as soft determinism. Compatibilists may also argue that determinism is irrelevant to the experience of freedom and moral choice – this is the position expressed in section b) above.

  Hume was a compatibilist. His empirical description of the laws of nature distinguishes between laws as *commands* and laws as *descriptions*. The laws of nature are descriptive: they do not say that something *must* happen, only that it has always been observed to happen. Causality does not entail necessity; we cannot be certain of the future on the basis of observation of the past. Hence Hume was able to accept the principle of causality without denying that we have free will.

Note:

A detailed survey of these positions, and of their limitations, is given in Honderich's book, *How Free are You?* In particular, it is important to distinguish between those (e.g. David Hume and G E Moore) who emphasised freedom in terms of seeing a person's inner motivation as *one of* the causes of an event and those (e.g. Kant) who saw freedom as a person's ability to originate an entirely new causal series – a freedom based on pure reason, not an option prompted by existing natural wants.

3 How free do I need to be?

> **KEY ISSUE**   To make sense of ethics, we need sufficient freedom to act and take responsibility for our actions.

From the previous section we have seen that the experience of freedom is an essential condition for moral choice. We have also seen that the reductionist argument – that we have no freedom whatsoever – is irrelevant, because it still leaves us with the fact of the experience of freedom and choice and the need to understand and evaluate such choices. But we also noted that we are all conditioned in some way. There are influences on our decision-making and on the moral rules that prevail in various societies. If we were completely free of all external causes and conditions, we would never stop to think about what we 'ought' to do, because we would never be influenced by anything that might suggest one course of action rather than another. *To make sense of ethics, we need sufficient freedom to act, and take responsibility for our actions, in the context of a finite range of possible courses of action.*

There are limitations on my freedom:

- Physical limitations: I cannot be morally required to do something of which I am physically or mentally incapable. (On the other hand, if I choose to put myself into a situation where I am physically incapable – e.g. if drunk or drugged – then I can be considered to be morally responsible for my condition and therefore for whatever happens as a result of it, which would not have happened had I been sober.)
- Legal and social limitations: If the law prevents me from doing something, then I cannot be blamed for not doing it. Of course, this assumes that obeying the law is the right thing to do, which depends upon the nature of the society which has produced that law. If a society is judged to be unjust, then there may be a moral case to be made for deliberately breaking the law. Even where there are no specific laws, social conditioning can have the same effect.
- Personal and psychological limitations: A psychotherapist or analyst, observing my present behaviour, thoughts and anxieties, may seek to find their origins in early experience or trauma. My ability to function as a mature adult may be limited by my past experiences.
- A religious believer may claim that his or her actions are directed by God, either by God having organised circumstances in order to bring about His chosen course of action, or by requiring the believer to obey His commandments. The believer may not feel that he or she is free to oppose God's will.

The above are general limitations on my freedom, but what about those specific limitations when I act under orders? The twentieth century provided a host of examples of political systems that were widely considered to be evil on the grounds of their disregard for individual human rights. Some of those who acted on behalf of such regimes were subsequently accused of crimes against humanity, but argued that they were not guilty because they were simply following orders.

Example
The killing of unarmed civilians or the humiliation of prisoners of war raises these issues, as does the 'ethnic cleansing' of areas by invading troops. Take the example of a soldier or prison guard who

is ordered to 'soften up' a prisoner prior to interrogation. It may be argued that a person has a duty to disobey a command that is obviously wrong, since it involves actions deemed unlawful under international law. In this case there is a conflict of loyalty – with individual conscience and international law on one side and military authority on the other. The soldier may be physically able to disobey such an order, but may believe that it is in the general interest of ending the conflict that he should obey the command and cause this particular individual to suffer. He may face severe punishment if he disobeys. In such a situation, is the soldier actually free? Is a natural fear of punishment a sufficiently strong argument to justify the claim that he was not free to disobey?

But if that is the case, then what about soldiers in a battle? If a soldier is ordered to attack some enemy position, even though it appears almost certain that he will be killed in the attempt, he is expected to obey that order, and it would generally be regarded as right and honourable for him to do so. Surely, the soldier's action in disobeying an illegal order (e.g. to kill civilians or humiliate prisoners), in spite of the personal consequences, should similarly be counted as right and honourable.

A soldier who always stops to consider whether it is morally right for him to obey an order is not going to survive long in the armed services. Does that mean that people under political or military authority have thereby surrendered such a measure of freedom that they can no longer be held responsible for the actions they perform? In this military example, those concerned were conscious, and were in a situation where rational thought and choice could have been made, but they claimed that they were (in effect) merely instruments (although conscious ones), acting on behalf of others. They therefore considered that they could not be held responsible for the actions they carried out, since they were not given sufficient freedom to enable them to be responsible.

a) Internal and external freedom

It is important to distinguish between an internal freedom that a person has and the external restraints imposed on him or her. As we saw above, there are many factors that stop me behaving exactly as I might wish. I know rationally that there would be serious consequences from certain actions and therefore that it cannot be in my best interests to do them. Equally, I might value the freedom (e.g. freedom from prison) which I can enjoy if I do not break the law.

Thus, for example, in the UK, I am not free to drive on the right-hand side of a single carriageway road, and I accept that the view of society is that it is wrong to steal. On the other hand, I could *imagine* driving on the wrong side of the road whilst escaping with stolen goods. *I have an internal freedom to think about alternatives and decide what I wish to do.*

It is these situations that provide the various moral dilemmas because, if everyone automatically wanted what was allowed by external authority, there would be no problem. The problem is that internal freedom allows us to want. Hence I may have a strong inclination to break the law in some way. I feel that I am free to want to do it, even if it is something that I cannot get away with. I may also decide that it would be responsible to curb my freedom for the benefit of society.

There are many external freedoms offered by society, for example, freedom of speech, or of religious beliefs and practices, freedom from arbitrary arrest, or the freedom of equal treatment under the law. These can be laid down by legislation. Other freedoms simply express the possible freedom of the individual to operate within society. Thus there is the freedom offered by education or freedom from poverty, or the economic freedom to work and accumulate wealth. A 'free' society is one that claims to offer as much personal autonomy as possible. On the other hand, all societies place restrictions on external freedoms, otherwise they could not function. I cannot be free to take everything as my own without thereby restricting the freedom of others. Therefore all external freedom is a matter of social compromise.

b) Inner freedom and responsibility

The term 'responsible' is used in two ways. You can be said to be responsible for something if you are the person who did it. Daubing graffiti on a police station may be something for which you are held responsible. That is not the same as saying that, in doing so, you were acting responsibly. In this second use of the word, you are 'responsible' when you are old enough to understand the meaning of freedom and law, and you are able to control your behaviour. To be responsible (in this second sense) is not the same thing as being obedient. You may come to the conclusion that a law needs to be changed, and that the only way of bringing that to people's attention is to break the law. In such a case, being morally responsible requires disobedience.

Moral 'responsibility' in the first sense of the word means:

● that you are the person who did something;
● that you were conscious at the time (or had consciously chosen to render yourself unconscious);
● that you could have acted differently but chose not to do so.

In the second sense, 'responsibility' requires:

● the acceptance of free will;

- the acceptance of rational norms;
- the balance of individual, social and universal moral criteria.

In other words, to claim that you are acting responsibly requires you to take 'responsibility' for what you are doing; you cannot claim, at one and the same time, to be morally responsible and also incapable of making a free choice. Nor can you claim to be responsible if you cannot, at least in theory, give a justification for your actions. To say 'I just felt like it' is not a moral justification. Equally, moral responsibility implies that you can weigh up the values by which you choose to live and can assess the extent to which these conform to both the immediate social and legal rules and the wider demands of universal moral norms.

Note:
Those studying Hinduism or Buddhism may want to consider the role of *karma* in a discussion of moral freedom. Every action generates *karma*, either good or bad, which in turn influences for good or ill the context for future actions and choices. Since it is argued that the effects of earlier *karma* can be overcome by moral actions in the present, *karma* cannot be said to determine present action (otherwise there would be no way of improving one's situation), merely to provide the context in which present choices are made (i.e. it is 'compatibilist').

---

c) The concept of 'freedom'

In his book, *Living Philosophy*, Ray Billington sets out the problems associated with considering freedom as a concept. It is sometimes assumed that there is something called 'freedom' out there that can be discussed and that might or might not exist – such as when we discuss the relationship between causality and personal freedom. He suggests quite simply that there would be no 'problem' of freedom if people were not free! It is because we experience and know what freedom is that we feel we have a problem; hence Billington takes the view that arguments about the existence of moral freedom are pointless, since everyone knows what it is to be free.

This view is an important one, since it shows that issues of determinism and reductionism are as meaningless in a world where everyone experiences freedom as discussions about the possibility of sight would be (to use his own example) in a world in which nobody was blind. Hence the danger of taking 'freedom' to be a concept and then debating whether or not it exists.

4 Is and ought

We shall see later that the philosopher David Hume complained that many people started to describe what 'is' and then slipped into speaking about what 'ought' to be done, without explaining why they had done so. This point was the basis of a major criticism of ethical theories made by G E Moore (1873–1958) in *Principia Ethica* (1903), one of the most influential books on ethics in modern times. He called the attempt to derive an 'ought' from an 'is' the **naturalistic fallacy**.

The general point here is that 'is' describes the facts of a situation. Those facts are generally regarded as morally neutral. They only become part of moral debate when, in response to them, someone says what 'ought' to be done.

Thus, for example, that children are starving as a result of famine is in itself morally neutral. It simply describes the condition of those who die for lack of food. It only becomes a matter of moral debate once, in response to this, it can be shown that a person is able to rectify the situation but has chosen not to do so. Therefore: 'Children are starving' may lead someone to say, 'You ought to do something to help them'. But the second does not follow logically from the first. There has to be a further stage, in the form of a **maxim** (or moral principle), which comes into play. In this case the maxim would be: 'Where there is suffering that can be relieved, it should be relieved'. Once that is inserted, the second of the statements is seen as a consequence of the first. But that maxim cannot simply be proved with reference to facts. It is an interpretation and evaluation of the facts.

In other words: *Ethics is largely concerned with those maxims, laws or agreements that enable 'ought' statements to be made in response to 'is' statements.*

In terms of presenting an ethical argument, one must therefore be on guard against presenting it simply in terms of what 'is' the case. Descriptions of situations, however horrific, do not in themselves count as an argument for a moral point of view. For the argument to be ethical, it has to contain (or hint at, or imply) statements about the principles upon which the moral judgement is being made. Without such principles, there is no justification of subsequent 'ought' statements. Therefore, in examining any argument, check:

- the facts that are to be considered;
- the principles upon which the moral argument is to be based;
- the application of those principles to this particular situation.

If any one of those three is missing, the argument will not be sound. Where conclusions differ, it is important to go back and check the principles upon which they are based, as well as the facts they address.

5 The absolute and the relative

Some people argue objectively. They use logic to reach conclusions from the facts they present. The conclusions reached by such an argument will be true if:

- the facts are correct;
- the logic of the argument is sound.

Other people argue subjectively. They present their views and show why they follow from fundamental values that they hold. They may use objective facts in presenting their case; they may use logic to get from their values to their specific moral conclusions; but fundamentally the argument depends upon agreement with the personal views and values expressed. If you do not accept these, you are unlikely to agree with the conclusions.

In fact, most moral issues involve a blending of both objective and subjective elements. The desire to present a moral argument suggests that what is being argued for has broader application than a mere expression of personal preference. In that case, it will need to be presented with some kind of agreed logic, and will also need to be supported by facts. On the other hand, most moral arguments may be reduced to a discussion of fundamental personal values – which are clearly subjective. The situation is also coloured by the argument that one cannot get an 'ought' from an 'is' and therefore that no amount of factual information is going to be sufficient to decide whether something is objectively right or wrong.

If there are objective moral principles, then it should be possible to express them in such a way that you can say that a certain action will be wrong for everyone, not just for the person whose situation you are considering. Indeed some have claimed (e.g. Kant, see page 97) that one should be willing for the principle upon which one decides to act, to become a universal law. The more ethics is based on reason and objectivity, the more it tends to claim to offer absolute and universal principles. How does this square with the observed fact that no two situations are ever exactly the same?

a) Social variety and ethical relativism

It is quite obvious that circumstances make an enormous difference to what is considered right or wrong. For example, to kill someone you love in order to spare them the pain, discomfort or humiliation of living through the last days of a progressive, incurable and debilitating disease, is quite different from killing a stranger in the course of a robbery. The morality of that action is 'relative' to the situation and the motives of the person concerned.

But there is a more general issue raised by moral relativism. It is generally believed today that everyone is entitled to his or her views and the freedom to express them. One might not agree with what a person is saying, but one can defend the right of that person to say it. It can therefore be argued that observing different social customs and values in different societies leads to moral relativism – what is right in one society would be wrong in another. What is important here is to understand the fundamental principles that underlie social differences. One might then look at people whose moral views differ from one's own and try to see the world from their point of view.

Example

Take the example of polygamy. In a culture where there is a shortage of men (as a result of warfare, for example) and many widows who receive no support from society in general, it might be considered appropriate for those men who can afford to do so to take the widows as additional wives and support them. This was the situation in the early days of the Muslim community, for example. Polygamy is therefore the direct result of a fundamental view that women should be cared for and protected.

On the other hand, a view that polygamy is wrong can be taken on exactly the same grounds – namely that men have sexual appetites that outstrip their ability to care for and support the various women whom they might wish to marry. Women are protected by insisting that a man shall have only one wife.

Here we see a single value being used as the basis for moral arguments that lead to opposite conclusions. The reason is that the circumstances are very different. Do we have cultural relativity here or do we have absolutist ethics? The answer to this is not simple. With respect to the final action that is taken, we have cultural relativity; with respect to the fundamental values and principles, we have an absolutist moral principle that it is right to protect those who are vulnerable.

The key difference between moral absolutism and a relativist approach is that the latter is prepared to accept that there is in general no way to establish absolute principles and values, but that both value and principle are given from within a social setting. In other words, we need to ask: Are values and moral principles *expressed through* particular societies and their laws, or are they *created by* those societies and their laws?

The true relativist is one who takes a 'created by' approach. The 'expressed through' view may accommodate an absolutist view, i.e. that there is a universal principle, but its implementation will be culturally determined.

Ethics looks at the bases upon which moral judgements are made. It is therefore possible that the same ethic may be expressed differently through different cultures. It is not even necessary to argue that a moral principle can be expressed in a way that is independent of all cultures, simply that those principles can be shared across cultures. They are likely to be based on those things that are not culturally dependent. In other words, on a fundamental understanding of human nature, or basic human needs.

Keep in mind that …
A relativist will generally hold at least one absolute rule, namely that it is wrong to impose absolute rules.
This is because most ethical thinkers who are sensitive to cultural and social differences want to ensure that the autonomy of the individual is respected. It is seen as wrong to impose one cultural norm of behaviour on those who come from a different culture. In other words, one may argue, 'I disagree with you, but I maintain that it is your right to disagree with me'.

b) Moral relativism and cultural relativism

It may be valuable to distinguish between 'moral relativism' – the belief that there are no moral absolutes, and that everything depends on particular circumstances – and a more general 'cultural relativism', which simply claims that a person's views and choices are relative to the society in which they live.

To some extent, everyone accepts a measure of cultural relativism. It would be nonsense to expect people who are brought up differently to have exactly the same moral sensibilities. One might argue, from the standpoint of one's own culture, that another culture approves of things of which one's own culture disapproves, and that those things are therefore morally wrong. But that begs the question of whether someone in that culture is morally justified in going along with the values of that culture, or, indeed, whether he or she is ever really free to go against them.

A cultural relativism may still hold that there are certain qualities – virtues such as honesty, kindness, loyalty and altruism – that can be displayed in a great variety of ways by different people in different cultures. Such a view is compatible with the claim that there are basic moral principles, however differently they may be expressed in different cultures.

c) Intrinsic evil

To say that there can be absolute moral judgements implies that some things are intrinsically good and others intrinsically evil. In other words, that there are values that can be applied to all people at all times and in all places. Thus you could say that the killing of innocent human life is an intrinsic evil. This would be based on a general concept of the value of life. A person guilty of some terrible crime (it might be argued) needs to be killed in order to protect society, either directly or indirectly. Therefore one needs to specify 'innocent'.

Of course, this could be extended. Vegetarians might argue that the killing of innocent animal life is also an intrinsic evil. In this case, it is a principle based on a general concept of the value of all life, animal as well as human.

Thus, if you can establish that there are certain things that you consider to be intrinsically evil, it follows that there will be absolute moral principles as a result. On the other hand, if you believe that nothing is evil in itself, but only that it is judged to be so by the conventions of a particular society at a particular time, then you will accept only relativist moral arguments.

Alternatively, if you hold that it is always right to allow every society to decide what shall be right or wrong, rather than impose on them an external criterion of morality, it implies that you see the imposition of one person's values on another as an intrinsic evil.

It may even be argued that it is society itself that generates evil. Jean-Jacques Rousseau – the philosopher whose political ideas influenced the French Revolution, but who also had considerable influence on thinking about education and society – believed that everyone started life innocent, but became corrupted by society. In other words, if there were no temptations, no sense of the value of money, of status, etc., there would be no envy, no lust for the goods of others and hence no theft.

Those who argue for absolute moral standards also tend to argue that everyone is responsible for his or her choices. The more relativist thinkers, following Rousseau, asserted that bad behaviour can be accounted for by the range of temptations and corrupting influences offered by society.

Summary List

- Morality is concerned with the free choice of rational human beings.
- Human freedom is experienced in spite of arguments that everything is totally conditioned or reduced to its physical components.
- Our freedom is always limited by internal and external constraints.
- We cannot argue from an 'is' to an 'ought'.
- Social and cultural variety influence the moral evaluation of actions and may lead to 'relativism'.
- A key for distinguishing absolutist from relativist ethics is whether anything may be considered to be intrinsically evil.

Questions

1. **a)** Explain how the idea of cause and effect can lead to the view that all events are determined. Do you think this view undermines the idea of moral action? Give your reasons.

    or b) The more we know another person, the better we can predict how he or she will react in any given situation. Does such knowledge suggest that, if everything were known about a person, his or her experienced freedom of action would be an illusion? Discuss.

2. Explain with examples why one should not try to derive an 'ought' from an 'is' (the naturalistic fallacy). What is needed in order to justify a statement about what one 'ought' to do?

3. Should each society or culture decide what is right or wrong? If so, can one society or culture ever judge the moral values of another? What effect does such cultural relativity have on the idea of individual moral responsibility? Illustrate your answer with examples of situations where an individual might be tempted to act against the values of his or her society or culture.

Discussion Topics

- Are determinism and free will incompatible?
- If I experience freedom, does that mean that I am free?
- If people are not free to make moral choices, should we punish criminals?

The above topics are broadly based, but give scope for a serious analysis and discussion of basic options in terms of hard or soft determinism/compatibilism.

4 Moral Language

KEYWORDS

moral – behaviour that conforms to an accepted set of norms

immoral – behaviour that goes against an accepted set of norms

amoral – action that is not seen as morally significant by the person performing it

teleological – an approach to ethics based on the expected end or purpose of an action

logical positivism – the view that for language to be meaningful it must be verifiable by sense experience

metaphysical ethics – theories relating ethics to an overall view of the universe

intuitionism – the theory that 'good' can be recognised but not defined

emotivism – the view that ethical statements are merely expressions of approval or disapproval

prescriptivism – the view that ethical statements prescribe a course of action

Before examining moral arguments, it is important to clarify some of the basic terms that are used. Exact definitions are not needed at this point, simply because they will depend on the arguments being examined. So, for example, if you are looking at an argument that says that goodness and right action are based on 'X', then the meaning of 'good' will depend on what that 'X' is. If you try to define 'good' before looking at the argument, then you have pre-judged its conclusion!

So, in this chapter, we shall look in general at some of the key words used in ethics, and we will then examine the claim that all moral language is meaningless, and at some of the ways in which philosophers have tried to justify its use. This study of the nature of ethical statements (as opposed to the study of particular arguments or moral claims) is termed meta-ethics.

1 Some ethical terms

a) Ethics and morals

Although these two words are derived from the Greek and Latin forms of the same concept, a distinction is sometimes made between them. For example, it is sometimes said that ethics is to do with theory and morals with practice, or that ethics is concerned with general issues and morality with specific cases.

Some might claim that ethics is the accepted set of norms of behaviour for a particular society or group, whereas morality refers to choices that are based on values that are imposed from outside the social group, chiefly from religious or philosophical beliefs. This distinction is not generally helpful, since any set of values or principles of conduct that are accepted as the ethic of a group or profession must ultimately rest on fundamental beliefs about the nature of life. In other words, your 'ethic' (in the narrow sense of that word), if it is not just an arbitrary acceptance of a set of rules, must ultimately be based on a sense of right and wrong and on the values that give rise to such a sense. And this, of course, is what morality is about, whether or not its arguments are associated with religious concepts or come about by agreement between individuals in society.

Another distinction is sometimes made, namely that your morals are shown in what you do and your ethics are the rational justification you give for what you do. This is implied by the term 'moral philosophy', which is interchangeable with 'ethics'. Ethics is the rational examination of morals. But that does not mean that morality and ethics can be separated from one another. An action that is unconscious, or in which the agent has no free choice, is not generally considered to be morally significant. Morality is concerned with action that is the result of choice, and which is therefore open to justification, praise or blame. In other words, once you are in a position to say that an action is morally significant, it has already become the subject of ethical debate.

It is possible that the attempt to define the term 'ethics' and distinguish it from 'morals' was an attempt to get away from a narrow sense of morality, associated particularly in Western minds with religious sanctions concerning sexual activity, and the term 'immorality' still has that connotation.

In this book, the terms 'moral' and 'ethical' will equally be used for arguments concerning right and wrong, the norms of activity that result from such arguments, and the actions that display or go counter to such norms. On the other hand, *if a distinction is to be made between the two terms, it is that ethics is used to describe the rational and systematic examination of moral issues.*

It is also important to distinguish between three terms:

- *Moral*
  To behave morally is to conform to a set of ethical norms, whether these are personal, religious or established by a group or profession.
- *Immoral*
  To be immoral is to go against a professed set of norms. Notice, however, that an action may be immoral according to one set of norms and moral according to another. For example, consider people who are starving and therefore steal in order to feed themselves and their families. On one level it can be argued that theft is wrong. But it could equally be argued that there is a prior moral requirement to save life, and that the institution of private property should come second to this – and therefore that it is right to steal if that is the only means of saving life.
- *Amoral*
  An action is amoral, with respect to the person who performs it, if it is done without reference to any moral perspective, or to any values that could give rise to a moral perspective. For example, a cat playing with a terrified mouse prior to killing it is acting amorally, simply because a cat has no sense of right or wrong. The same could be claimed for a human who is suffering from a mental condition such that he or she is incapable of understanding the meaning of right and wrong, or incapable of experiencing the emotions that would normally be associated with – for example – inflicting pain on others.

b) Good and bad/right and wrong

The most basic word in ethics is also the most difficult to define. Indeed, it is because it is so difficult to define the meaning of 'good' that we have so many problems in ethics. We all have some sense of what it means, but that meaning is extremely difficult to specify accurately.

A dictionary definition of 'good' (e.g. in *The Concise Oxford Dictionary*) may start with 'having the right qualities, satisfactory, adequate', but it will then go on to give a very large number of contextual meanings – 'good works', 'good will', 'good time', etc. – in order to show the scope of its use. The need to give all those different contexts shows just how varied the meaning can be. The same dictionary defines 'bad' as 'worthless', 'inferior, deficient', 'of poor quality', 'incorrect, not valid; counterfeit or debased', 'unpleasant' and so on, each related to a particular context.

This great variety of uses of the terms 'good' and 'bad' raises some fundamental questions for ethics:

- Is 'goodness' something that exists in things independently of our deciding that they are good? In other words: is goodness an inherent quality?
- Or is it something that we determine by an act of will? Do I call something good simply because I approve of it? Is its goodness related to its usefulness to me?
- Is goodness in any sense absolute, or does it depend on each person's view?
- If goodness is related to our perception, rather than being an inherent quality, do we have any means of deciding the issue when one person calls something 'good' and another calls it 'bad'?
- What have a good knife and a good opera singer in common? What is it that enables them both to be termed 'good'?

These are questions that will need to be explored further in terms of the various ethical theories. And, of course, we cannot get far with definitions of 'right' and 'wrong' unless we first know what we mean by 'good'.

As a starting point, perhaps, one could think about the approach taken by the Greek philosopher Aristotle. He saw goodness in terms of each thing fulfilling the purpose for which it had been designed. Thus a good knife is a knife that cuts well. So what is a good human being? Clearly, in order to know the answer to that, you have to understand what a human being is designed to do or be. This led to the Natural Law approach to ethics, which we shall examine later.

On the other hand it is possible to give some external justification for calling something good. Thus, for example, a religious person might say that 'good' is whatever God commands.

A useful distinction is made between deontological and **teleological** approaches: If you consider the rules that govern human activity, with issues of right and wrong, then you are taking a *deontological* approach – in other words, an approach based on a sense of 'duty'. If you think instead about the chosen goal that is sought in an action, or the 'good' at which life aims, then you are taking a *teleological* approach – in other words, one based on the expected 'end'.

It is clear, therefore, that in ethics you cannot simply define your terms and then expound ethical theories by straightforward, logical deduction. Every theory or approach to ethics will, by its very nature, redefine the meaning of the fundamental terms it uses. The words make sense in the context of a theory or overall view of life. Once removed from that context, they become vague and almost impossible to define. But before we look at the theories that explore what is good and right, there are two prior questions to be examined: Do moral statements make sense at all? What are they actually doing?

We will examine these questions now in terms of theories of moral language that have been developed in the twentieth century, in response to the challenge that moral language is not factual and is therefore meaningless.

2 Can moral claims be justified?

a) Logical positivism

Much of twentieth-century ethics has been bound up with meta-ethical questions – in other words, with questions about the meaning and justification of ethical language itself, rather than with matters concerning what is actually right or wrong.

The main reason for this was the development of **logical positivism**, a view of language that limited its meaning to that which could be verified by sense experience. In other words, if I make a statement, it is either true or false depending on whether someone could in principle go and check the facts to which I refer. If there is no possible evidence that can be given either for or against that statement being true, then it is meaningless. This approach was summed up as: *The meaning of a statement is its method of verification.* In other words, to say 'X exists' means 'If you go and look, you will see X'.

This view of language is found in the early work of Wittgenstein. His *Tractatus* (1921) was an immensely influential book, which inspired the work of a group of philosophers known as the Vienna Circle, and it was there that logical positivism developed. Its influence was spread by the publication in 1936 of *Language, Truth and Logic* by A J Ayer. Ayer claimed that there were only two kinds of propositions:

- truths known by definition (e.g. mathematics and logic)
- truths known through sense experience (i.e. proved by external facts)

Where do moral statements come in such a scheme? If they are known by definition then they are mere tautologies, claiming nothing. On the other hand, how can you point to facts that prove a moral statement? That, too, is impossible, as we saw above in the argument that you cannot derive an 'ought' from an 'is'. Hence, Ayer saw all moral statements as meaningless.

This challenge dominated ethics from the 1930s until the 1960s, and we shall examine a number of attempts that were made to find a meaning for ethical statements that would not be dismissed by Ayer's argument. But in order to appreciate the impact of positivism, it is useful to look at two approaches to ethics that preceded it: **metaphysical ethics** and **intuitionism**.

b) Metaphysical ethics

'Metaphysical ethics' wanted to show that morality could be related to an overall view of the world and the place of humankind within it. F H Bradley, in *Ethical Studies* (1876), argued that the supreme good for humankind was self-realisation. In other words, we act in a way that is morally good when we do those things that allow us to develop ourselves as part of a wider community. Morality is therefore not just about particular actions, but about the character of the people who perform them, and the understanding they have of their part in the wider world.

Now, metaphysical ethics of this sort depends on two abstract ideas: the world as a whole, and self-realisation. Neither of these can be reduced to the sort of evidence that the logical positivists were later to claim as necessary for meaning. Thus, they would have seen metaphysical ethics as meaningless.

c) Intuitionism

G E Moore argued in *Principia Ethica* (1903) that the primary term 'good' could not be defined. He did so in the context of claiming that most earlier ethical theories had fallen into the naturalistic fallacy of trying to derive an 'ought' from an 'is' (see page 25). He came to the conclusion that goodness was not a natural property – you could not equate it with anything else, or give a description of it in terms of other things. You may know what 'good' is, but you cannot define it. Fundamental moral principles are therefore known by intuition. They cannot be proved to be true or false, but are recognised as soon as they are thought about. Thus we know what it means to say that something is 'good', even to say that many different things are good, although we cannot point to any particular quality that makes it so. The analogy Moore used was with colour: *We know what 'yellow' is, and can recognise it wherever it is seen, but we cannot actually define yellow. In the same way, we know what 'good' means, but cannot define it.*

Starting from the indefinable 'good', Moore's book raises two basic questions:

- What things should exist for their own sake?
  His answer: those that we call intrinsically good.
- What actions ought we to perform?
  His answer: those that produce most good.

Now, in contrast to metaphysical ethics, this approach does not depend on any abstract concepts about the world as a whole. On the other hand, 'good' is not simply a word we choose to apply to objects, but is the name of a quality that inheres in things. Moore thought of good as something rather like 'beautiful' – a quality that could be found in things but not described. This approach came to be known as *intuitionism*, although that was not a term that Moore himself used for it.

In a further development of this approach, H A Prichard (1871–1947) argued that you could not reduce moral obligation to anything else. Like Moore's 'good' it was something known directly by intuition (Prichard's work on this, *Moral Obligation*, was published in 1949).

Another Oxford philosopher influenced by Moore, W D Ross (1877–1971), argued in *The Right and the Good* (1930) and *The Foundations of Ethics* (1939) that Moore was right to deny that you could equate goodness with any natural property (the naturalistic fallacy – no 'ought' from an 'is'), but that he was wrong in arguing that the only criterion for moral obligation was to maximise the good. Rather, he pointed out that one may have a conflict of duties, and it may not be at all obvious which is to take priority. My duty is therefore self-evident (known through intuition) provided that it does not conflict with another self-evident duty.

Notice what is implied by the intuitionist approach: you cannot use any factual evidence to show that something is good or that one has a moral obligation. All basic moral judgements are self-evident.

d) Meaningless?

It will now be clear why the logical positivist position was so threatening to ethics. If meaning is only given with respect to the evidence provided by the senses, then metaphysical ethics is meaningless, since it is based on abstract concepts that do not have a 'cash value' in terms of experience. But the attempt to escape from that charge and claim that morality is known through intuition is equally threatened. For if goodness and obligation cannot be 'reduced' to evidence of any sort, then – as far as the logical positivists were concerned – they too were meaningless. The positivists hoped to put language and meaning on the same sure basis as the physical sciences. Everything had to be tested out in terms of evidence: no evidence, no meaning.

The key feature here is the naturalistic fallacy mentioned in Chapter 3. If we can never argue from an 'is' to an 'ought', then any approach to language that tries to base meaning on evidence must automatically rule out the possibility of meaningful ethics.

But the positivist claim went further. Wittgenstein (and others) argued that *we can have no knowledge of private mental states*. They argued that to describe someone as angry, for example, did not imply that one had special access to a mental state. Rather, the word 'angry' describes someone who is red in the face, shouting, waving a fist in the air, and so on. Anger 'means' all that, because that is the only way in which I can specify why I used that word to describe that person. To take another example: an itch, in this theory, is merely a disposition to scratch. Wanting to scratch is what we call 'having an itch'. There is no itch independent of the disposition to scratch.

Faced with such criticism, attempts were made to find a meaning for religious language that would satisfy the criteria for meaningfulness set by logical positivism.

e) Emotivism

The criticism of moral statements by the logical positivists was based on the assumption that such statements were making factual claims. A J Ayer argued for a theory about the nature of ethical statements that became known as **emotivism**. An emotivist view gets round the logical positivist rules about what is meaningful by claiming that moral statements are not factual, but express the feelings of the person who makes them. If you like something, then you call it 'good', if you dislike it, 'bad'. Thus two people can consider exactly the same facts and come to quite different moral conclusions. One cannot say that one is right or the other is wrong, because there are no facts that separate them; one can only accept that each is using moral judgements to express his or her emotional response to that set of facts.

This approach was taken by C L Stevenson in his book, *Ethics and Language* (1944). He was particularly concerned about how moral statements are used, and what results they are intended to produce. He claimed that the word 'good' was a persuasive definition; it was there to express your emotions. On the other hand, if you tried to go on from there to give some reason why you felt that way, that is more than emotivism will allow.

One key question to ask in considering this theory is: How do emotions expressed in 'moral' statements differ (if at all) from other emotions? If moral statements are simply a listing of how we feel, that does not seem to do justice to the way in which moral statements are actually used. I may sense that, when I say of something that it is right or good, I am doing more than simply describing my emotions at the time. What more am I doing when I make moral statements? Let us move to consider a second theory.

f) Prescriptivism

Another approach to the same problem is to say that to make a moral statement is to prescribe a particular course of action. This approach was taken by R M Hare (*The Language of Morals*, 1952, and *Freedom and Reason*, 1963). He argued that a moral statement is 'prescribing' a course of action, recommending that something should be done, not just expressing a feeling. On the other hand, moral statements are rather more than commands. A command is simply a request to do a particular thing at a particular moment, whereas a moral statement is making a more general suggestion about what action should be taken. In other words, a moral statement is both *prescriptive* and also *universalisable*: stating what everyone should do in the circumstances. Hare believed that, in this way, it was possible to apply reason and logic to matters of value.

> 'If I ought to do this, then somebody else ought to do it to me in precisely similar circumstances.' So I have to ask myself: 'Am I prepared to prescribe that somebody else should do it to me in like circumstances?'
>
> *R M Hare in Bryan Magee,* Men of Ideas *(1978)*

Prescriptivism suggests that in responding to moral statements, we do not acknowledge that they are either true or false, but simply accept or reject the actions they are prescribing. Thus you may say to me 'It is right to feed those who are starving'. If I agree with that statement, what I am actually saying is 'Yes, and that is what I intend to do'.

All of this debate has come, of course, from the basic argument that you cannot derive an 'ought' from an 'is'. If (like the logical positivists) you believe that a statement only means something if you can point to evidence for it, where do you find your evidence for moral statements? Either in the area of human emotions expressed through them, or in the courses of action that such statements might prescribe – the first leads to emotivism and the second to prescriptivism.

Both theories avoid the claim that moral statements are meaningless, by pointing to the evidence of what actually happens when moral statements are made – for, whether or not they are meaningless in themselves, it is clear that moral statements do actually express emotions and recommend courses of action. In this, ethics moved in parallel with much linguistic philosophy in the first half of the twentieth century – away from a narrowly defined sense of meaning toward an appreciation of language that can be used in many different ways.

It is possible to argue that moral statements are means by which we overcome selfish perspectives. John Mackie (1917–81), in *Ethics: Inventing Right and Wrong* (1977), argued that:

- there are no objective moral values;
- therefore all moral claims are objectively 'false';
- but we can continue to use moral language if it helps us to overcome narrow views and sympathies.

In other words, Mackie was building on the work of emotivism and prescriptivism by saying that morality has a function but not an objective basis.

On the other hand, there is a fundamental question to ask of this approach: Why not enjoy having limited sympathies? Why bother with moral codes at all? Why should it make any difference if our views are completely selfish or universally benevolent? *If we are 'inventing' right and wrong, why are we doing it? What does humankind have to gain from having developed a sense of conscience? It would seem that at some point ethics needs to be based on something other than itself. Morality remains a phenomenon which needs some explanation.*

Two issues relate to this, but are beyond the scope of this present book. The first is nihilism. If there is no objective basis for ethical statements, and if they do no more than express our own preferences, then it is possible to argue that nothing whatever has inherent value. The second is that, if moral language simply refers to our present emotions or prescriptions, it is difficult to see how moral progress could be possible. What would it mean to say that I wanted to become a better person?

As was mentioned in the Introduction (see page 2), much discussion of ethics from the turn of the twentieth century to the 1960s was concerned with the attempt to find some meaning for ethical language. We need to keep such discussion in mind as we move now to consider some traditional ethical theories. Traditional theories are more concerned with finding a basis for moral values in experience, in emotions or in the way in which our minds work, than with meaning. In other words, they are concerned with questions such as 'What should I do?' and 'What is good?' rather than the secondary (meta-ethical) question 'What do I mean when I say that something is good?'.

Summary List

- The distinction was made between describing something as moral, immoral or amoral.
- There are two basic approaches to issues of right and wrong: the deontological (based on a sense of duty) and the teleological (based on expected results).
- Metaphysical ethics attempted to relate ethics to an overall view of the world.
- Intuitionism argued that 'good' could be known but not defined.
- Logical positivism challenged the meaningfulness of ethical language on the grounds that no empirical evidence could be given for its truth.
- Emotivism and prescriptivism attempted to avoid the logical positivist challenge by describing moral statements as either expressions of emotion or recommendations to take a particular course of action.

Questions

Revision activity

Most questions will link a consideration of ethical language to specific moral issues, so it is important to be able to recognise the various theories of language that are being used.

Consider the following statements:

1. It is always wrong to kill another human being.
2. Do whatever you feel will help you to develop as an individual; don't simply be guided by what other people think of you.
3. You should always consider other people's feelings, rather than your own.
4. It is right to steal food, if that is the only way to stay alive.

For each of these, say how you would interpret this statement from the standpoint of the theories of moral language set out in this chapter. In each case you should say also how you would decide whether or not to agree with the statement.

In other words, for statement 1, say how you would interpret it as an emotivist, and how (as an emotivist) you would decide whether to agree or not. Then go on to consider the same statement from the perspective of intuitionism, or prescriptivism. If you have already studied other ethical theories (e.g. utilitarianism, situation ethics etc.) it would be useful to include these in your assessment of the statements.

Essay question:

1. Moral statements are simply covert descriptions of emotions or recommendations for action. Discuss.

A good response to a question concerning the emotivist or prescriptivist theories of moral language should set them in the context of the challenge of logical positivism. In other words, it is important to show that these theories are responses to the undermining of the traditional bases for ethics.

Discussion Topic

● Does the emotivist theory degrade ethical discussion?

5 Plato and the Quest for Justice

KEYWORDS

episteme – Greek term for 'knowledge'

doxa – Greek term for 'opinion'

Form – a universal reality, in which individual things share

1 Introduction

In this chapter we shall be concerned with the idea of justice as it is explored within the *Republic*, and also with the basic idea of the Forms, and particularly the 'Form of the Good', which underlies the whole of Plato's philosophy.

Plato (*c.* 428–347 BCE) was born into a noble family in Athens, and much of his work shows an awareness of his political and social responsibilities, set against the background of the Greek city state (or *polis*). He was profoundly influenced by the philosopher Socrates, and when Socrates was condemned to death in 399 BCE, Plato left Athens. He returned in 387 BCE and founded the Academy, which may be considered the first university, by receiving students at his home.

Plato's writings generally take the form of dialogues (in which Socrates frequently appears as the principal character). They generally start with someone's claim to knowledge and the proposal of a definition of a key term. This is then scrutinised and tested by producing practical examples of its application, leading to the conclusion that the original definition was inadequate.

This 'Socratic' method aims to show the folly of superficial claims to knowledge, but implies that true knowledge is possible. Although the dialogues appear to be about the definition of terms, they are not simply about language, since it was Socrates' (and Plato's) conviction that language reflected reality, and therefore that a clarification of language was also a clarification of one's perception of reality. So when Plato discusses the meaning of justice, it is not merely the word 'justice' that is being considered, but the political reality that may be understood by that concept. Plato's early dialogues probably reflect the teachings of Socrates himself and generally follow the 'Socratic method' without appearing to present authoritative conclusions. Socrates made some fundamental points about virtue and morality, on which Plato was to build. They were:

- That virtue is knowledge: to know what is right is to do what is right.
- That all wrong-doing is the result of ignorance: nobody deliberately chooses to do what he or she knows to be wrong.

● That all virtues are fundamentally the same: you can't have one virtue but lack another.

The dialogues of the middle period (including the *Republic*) still have Socrates as the principal character, but increasingly Plato moves beyond the traditional 'Socratic' form, and starts to expound his own ideas – giving answers rather than simply asking questions – with other characters simply there to endorse what he is saying. There is also a change of emphasis, moving beyond ethical issues to examine the nature of reality itself. We have the development of his theory of Forms, in which Plato was to make a distinction between the appearance of things that are known to us through the senses, and underlying reality that makes them what they are, and which is known only through reason.

In an early dialogue (*Gorgias*), Plato enquires about what constitutes a person's supreme good. He examines the claims that it is the ability to persuade people so that one can get exactly what one wants, that it is the power of getting one's own way and that it is the ability to satisfy all one's desires. None of these proves to be adequate, and Socrates argues that a person's desires are endless, and therefore that one can never achieve complete satisfaction simply by being given what one desires. Rather, he argues that satisfaction has to be understood in terms of a form of life in which one could say exactly what was being desired. Thus Plato moves in the direction of saying that satisfaction comes through reason, not simply through giving way to the appetites.

A note on erotic love:

The *Symposium* discusses the nature of *eros* – the love that is also desire, craving for another (hence 'erotic' love). In it, the character of Aristophanes (who, in real life, was a comic poet who ridiculed Socrates, amongst others) presents the myth of human origins whereby in the past everyone had four arms and legs, being the equivalent of two people fixed together, but that people were then divided. Hence we all go through life sensing that we are incomplete, that there must exist somewhere another human being who will make us feel whole again.

Socrates suggests that the lover is in fact never satisfied, because the quest is actually for beauty and goodness itself. In other words, the quest is for something that is utterly beyond what any one good or beautiful person can offer.

The answer for Plato was to lie in the 'Form of the Beautiful' as that which, if we could once ascend to contemplate it, would completely satisfy us. The problem with this (pointed out by Alasdair MacIntyre in *A Short History of Ethics*, 1966) is that, in Plato's account, goodness and beauty are only known to a few educated individuals, whereas, in fact, everyone has *some* sense of what is good, for without it they would have nothing to desire or aspire to.

2 The *Republic*

The *Republic* is concerned with what is meant by justice. It takes the form of a Socratic dialogue in which various definitions are proposed and examined, but then moves on to a more systematic exposition of Plato's views of the ideal state, of the place of philosopher-rulers within it, the ethical principles needed to establish it and the fundamental nature of reality, which its rulers would need to understand in order to establish justice.

The proposal is presented by Thrasymachus, and then taken up by Glaucon and Adeimantus, that justice is what is in the interests of the stronger. Those who rule, in other words, determine what shall be considered just. There are differences between the proponents, in that Thrasymachus is crude in seeking to achieve his own ends in an obviously selfish way, whereas Glaucon and Adeimantus are prepared to be craftier and to accept moral principles and laws in order to achieve what they want in the long run.

They argue that, in a natural state, everyone is concerned for his or her own self-interest, but that society has to create a sense of order and justice in order to curb such self-interest for the benefit of others and to prevent total anarchy. People then obey the laws, since they fear the consequences of not doing so.

a) The ring of Gyges

But what if you could set aside all laws and act according to your own wishes and self-interest with guaranteed impunity? The story is told of the ring of Gyges, which had the power to make its wearer invisible. Given the opportunities afforded by such a ring, Gyges uses its power to achieve his own ends – in this case by seducing his queen and killing his king. The implication of the story is that, when all restraints and threats are removed, people will act in line with what they perceive to be their own self-interest. Adeimantus makes the point that, if someone is told to obey laws and to act justly, it is in order to achieve success – and therefore even acceptance of law is based on self-interest.

This part of the *Republic* raises a key feature of all social and political ethics, which is the conflict between individual self-interest and the general good. If you only consider individual self-interest, society breaks down. How then can you create a society that is ordered in such a way that everyone achieves appropriate satisfaction? This is Plato's quest.

3 The ideal ruler

KEY ISSUE   Plato argues that both the state and the individual should be ruled by reason.

Plato considers a society in which everyone's needs are to be met. He suggests that it will involve three different classes of people: workers, to produce the goods needed for society; the military, to defend the state; and rulers. Plato is convinced that people naturally fall into one or other of these three categories, and that it is best to divide the three functions between them, each taking what is most appropriate and sticking to that function alone.

So what makes a person a philosopher–king, capable of ruling the just state? Plato's answer is that the philosopher has knowledge (***episteme***) as opposed to opinion (***doxa***). If, for example, you are aware that a particular thing is beautiful, that is merely opinion, and you may well not be able to say why it is beautiful. On the other hand, if you are aware of the nature of beauty itself, the very essence of beauty, this in itself can become the object of knowledge, without depending upon particular examples.

Therefore the philosopher has knowledge of the essence of things – what Plato called the Forms – as opposed to the particulars that are encountered through our sense experience.

For Plato, knowledge of the **Forms** is achieved through reason rather than experience, and is therefore on firmer ground – we can be certain, because we can give a reasoned account of our knowledge. By contrast with this, you can never achieve certainty if your claim to knowledge is based solely on your experience of things – at most you can have opinion, since it is always liable to be challenged by yet another and differing experience.

If we say that two different things are beautiful, then we must have some concept of beauty, independent of the two examples before us, in order for that description to make sense.

Note:
There is a fundamental division in Plato's philosophy between eternal realities, which are known through reason, and the everyday world of particulars, which is known through sense experience. This dualism influences both his metaphysics (i.e. his theory about what exists) and his epistemology (i.e. his theory about how we can know what exists). It is also key to an understanding of his approach to ethics, because once he has established the importance of the eternal Forms he moves on to the central idea for his ethics – the 'Form of the Good'.

4 The account of the cave

KEY ISSUE   Plato argues that, to understand the Form of the Good, a person has to turn away from the puppet show of sense experience that most people take to be the whole of reality.

In Plato's famous analogy of the cave, prisoners sit in a cave facing its back wall. Behind them there is a fire, which casts shadows on the wall, caused by a succession of objects which are being carried to and fro behind the prisoners. They are unable to turn round and so cannot see either the objects or the fire. They therefore believe that the puppet show of shadows constitutes the whole of reality. If a prisoner is able to get free of his shackles, he can turn and see the fire and the objects moving before it. He now recognises that things that formerly seemed real are actually only shadows.

But that is not the end of the quest, for a prisoner who is able to get past the fire becomes aware that the cave has a mouth, and that beyond it is the light of the sun. This experience of looking into the sunlight is painful for him, since his eyes have become accustomed to seeing only the dull shadows within the cave. The sun becomes a transcendent source of goodness, energy and virtue. It cannot be defined, and it cannot even be looked at directly without pain, yet its presence gives light to all else. Thus, for Plato, the Form of the Good is the source of all values. But of course, once the former prisoner's eyes adjust to the daylight, it is difficult for him to return to the darkness of the cave, and indeed, if one challenged the reality of the shadows the result would be great resentment among those who think that the shadows are all that exists. Perhaps Plato saw Socrates in this light, suffering at the hands of those whose puppet show he had challenged.

The whole theory of Forms depends upon the idea that the Forms actually exist in another world (although not a world that can be perceived through the senses) and that we are born into this world with a vague memory of them – a memory that leads us to seek them, and enables us to use words like 'good' and 'beautiful' even when we cannot define them satisfactorily. This is Plato's way of overcoming the problem of how it is that we can speak of the Forms at all, as distinct from the particular things that are presented to our experience.

a) Implications of this metaphysics

In the analogy of the cave and elsewhere, it is clear that Plato's idea of goodness is transcendent. It is above and beyond any particular social conventions that concern people in their ordinary life. It may in fact be the source and inspiration for all other values, but it is a source that generally remains hidden. Whereas the other Forms, for

Plato, are an unchanging part of existence, the Form of the Good is beyond existence altogether. We cannot see it directly, although it gives meaning to all the other forms.

This is relevant to Plato's ethics. Knowledge of the Forms, and particularly the Form of the Good, is – for Plato – an end in itself. It gives meaning and purpose to life. And without some overall sense of meaning, moral considerations such as justice become meaningless. But there is another important issue here. Just as Socrates had said that virtue is knowledge, so Plato is arguing here that to do what is right, and to order society justly, is a matter of knowledge – not just knowledge of the individual things known to the senses (the shadows) but of the Form of the Good, which is known only through reason. If goodness and justice require reason, then philosophers should rule.

5 The ideal state

> **KEY ISSUE** Plato uses the analogy of the state to highlight three elements within the individual, with reason given the task of holding the appetites in check through the will.

For Plato, there are three classes of people:

- the rulers (or guardians)
- the auxiliaries (or military)
- the workers.

In order to have a state where the rulers, the auxiliaries and the workers each perform their own functions, Plato recognises that there must be propaganda to the effect that those who are to be workers are born as such and must accept their lot. Equally he is concerned that there should be careful selection and education in order to provide the guardians needed to rule the state.

It is essential that there be inequality of opportunity and education for Plato's state to work. He takes fairly drastic action in order to implement it. There is to be selective breeding, so that the healthiest and most intellectually gifted are able to produce more children. Marriages are sanctioned by the state, for the purpose of creating gifted rulers. The ages for childbearing are set down, and although sex is freely permitted outside that age range, any children of such unions must be eliminated either by abortion or infanticide. Similarly, all deformed children must be removed from society.

Children are to be removed from their parents and brought up and educated together, so that they do not know who their parents are – thus treating all with equal respect. Since children are not allowed to marry their own parents, all those whose age means that they could possibly be one's mother or father must be treated as such. In other words, in order to achieve the development of a ruling elite, Plato is prepared to sacrifice what others might see as fundamental individual rights and the natural family unit.

Once he establishes the means of training the guardians of his state, he has a system within which all three classes – guardians, auxiliaries and workers – know their place and work together in harmony.

Thus Plato outlines his ideal state, not because it is ever going to be possible to construct it, but simply in order to have a standard by which to judge actual states. So, having established his ideal, in which all sections of society work together, he traces the stages in the decline of such a state:

- *The timocratic state.* This is run by the military (the auxiliaries) rather than the philosopher–guardians. It is based on honour and respect for private property.
- *The oligarchy.* This is where society is run basically for the benefit of the ruling class, rather than for the benefit of all the citizens.
- The oligarchy breaks down when those who are oppressed rise up against the ruling class. This produces a *democracy*, where each claims an equal share of control over the state.
- Finally, since there will always be those who are dissatisfied with what they are able to achieve within a democracy, the system is taken over by a despot and the result is a *tyranny*.

Examples of all four types of state were found in Plato's day: Athens was a democracy, Sparta a timocracy, Corinth an oligarchy and Syracuse a tyranny. What Plato sought was what may be called an *aristocracy*, in modern terms a *meritocracy*. The rulers are those who, with the right training, are intellectually gifted enough to be able to establish justice. There is another important distinction between what Plato proposes and existing systems. In the latter, rulers act in a way that benefits themselves or their own class – this, indeed, had been Thrasymachus' position earlier in the *Republic*. The philosopher–guardians in Plato's state work for the benefit of others. Indeed, Plato points out that many people would prefer not to accept high office, since it is more pleasant to receive benefit from the rulers than to be in a position where one has constantly to be of service to others.

b) The nature of the self in this scheme

Plato sees the three types of citizen in his state as corresponding to three aspects of the self – *reason*, *will* and *appetite*.

The base elements in the human self are the appetites, corresponding to the workers. Plato clearly wanted to make sure that they were controlled. The human 'will', or spirited nature, exhibits emotions and takes action, corresponding to the auxiliaries in the state. Then finally there is rational self, which sees the balance that is needed and uses the will in order to control the appetites – the function of the rulers in a state.

Justice is achieved within the state when each class of people is able to perform its own function in harmony with the others. So also in an individual, the rational part is there to control the appetites and also to guide the spirited or wilful part that expresses itself in bravery and action. All three are acknowledged, but they are set in a very definite hierarchy. *In other words: appetites are to be controlled by reason, using the will to do so.*

The despot, as originally presented by Thrasymachus, is simply motivated by crude, unchecked appetite. He becomes the obvious alternative to the philosophical ruler, and thus to the person for whom reason rules in his or her life. On the other hand, the despot is shown in an extreme form, almost as a compulsive seeker of pleasure. Most people would not identify with such a 'despotic' state. For them, the quest for pleasure is modified in order to achieve satisfaction. This brings us to the next type – the crafty person who uses some measure of reason to control and direct his desires. Such a person is presented in the *Republic* by Glaucon and Adeimantus. He or she corresponds to the oligarchy or democracy, and is really the greater threat to Plato's ideal of the rational ruler than the cruder despot.

6 Why is it better to be just than unjust?

KEY QUESTION   Does the quest to satisfy the appetites inevitably lead to frustration?

Plato offers three reasons as to why this might be the case:

- A person who is unjust is ruled by his or her desires. But these are limitless and are therefore never to be satisfied – which results in frustration.
- If you know only your appetites, you are unable to judge between the benefits that reason can bring and those of the partial satisfaction of appetite. The philosopher, by contrast, knows both reason and appetite and is therefore in the best position to judge between them.
- Reason deals with eternal truths and values, whereas satisfying the appetites is only a temporary way of staving off a sense of loss or dissatisfaction. Therefore the values of reason are always to be preferred.

KEY QUESTION   In assessing these arguments of Plato's you need to consider whether or not he is right to have made this absolute distinction between reason and appetite. Do they actually work in opposition to one another as he suggests?

What Plato is desperate to show is that a just man has greater satisfaction, no matter how much of a failure he might appear to be in worldly terms (remember Socrates!), but that the person who is driven to worldly success will always remain unfulfilled, since appetites are boundless.

Towards the end of the *Republic*, Plato uses another myth, in which, after death, the just are rewarded and the unjust punished. Now this simply reflects his valuation of the two states, for it implies that the just deserve to be rewarded after death, rather than having justice as its own reward during this life. In a sense, therefore, the final myth does not actually contribute anything to Plato's argument for the inherent superiority of justice over injustice.

KEY ISSUE   Because Plato limits knowledge of justice to the philosophical few (the exceptional prisoner who escapes from the cave) there is always the danger that justice could be imposed by an intellectual elite upon a majority who are deemed to be incapable of understanding it.

Summary List

- Socrates held that virtue was knowledge, and therefore that wrong-doing was the result of ignorance.
- In the *Republic*, Plato considered various ideas about justice. He concluded that justice could be established in a person, as in a state, where reason held the appetites in check by means of the will.
- Plato considered the Form of the Good to be the source of all values. Insight into it qualified a person to rule, and gave a person an absolute by which all else could be judged.
- Hence being just (having one's life ordered by reason) is superior to being unjust because, without reason, the quest for the satisfaction of the appetites is bound to lead to frustration.

Questions

1. Knowledge automatically leads to virtue, and wrong-doing is the result of ignorance. Discuss these ideas, which Plato ascribes to Socrates, saying whether or not you agree with Socrates, and illustrating your discussion with examples from one or more present-day situations.

This question may serve to introduce the priority of the reason for Plato. It could also be related to the 'is' and 'ought' issue raised in the last chapter, in that knowledge (as it is commonly understood today) relates primarily to knowledge of facts, and that values are not discovered in the same way. This could then be contrasted with the broader idea of knowledge in Ancient Greece: for Plato, knowledge was not just knowing particular facts – shadows on the wall of the cave – but understanding reality itself.

2. If knowledge of the Forms is limited to an elite of philosophers, can it become a valid basis for morality? Discuss this challenge to Plato's ethics.

A possible criticism of Plato is that he is elitist, and that his theories allow a minority to rule the majority. In commenting on this, it might be as well to consider the social background against which Plato was writing. It raises broader issues about whether reason is the only basis upon which a moral approach to life can be built. Those who have already studies Hobbes and Rousseau, or utilitarianism, may come at this question from a broader perspective.

3. Is justice whatever is in the interests of the stronger? Discuss, with reference to Plato's *Republic*, illustrating your answer from modern political and ethical issues.

Discussion Topics

● Would Thrasymachus thrive today?
● Is it possible to persuade people of the 'myth' that they are born unequal, and therefore need to accept their given place in society? Is it equally a myth that all are born equal?
● Can your fundamental character be shaped by education and environment, as Plato implies by his programme of training for the guardians, or are you born with permanent character traits?

Note:
This last question might be debated in the light of the issue of freedom versus determinism outlined earlier.

6 Aristotle and Happiness

KEYWORDS

eudaimonia – Greek term for 'happiness'

telos – Greek term for 'end' or 'purpose'

the mean – Aristotle's idea that doing right involves a balance between extremes

logos – Greek for 'word', the universal rational principle in Stoic thought

In this chapter we shall explore Aristotle's idea of 'happiness' as the good to which all life aspires, looking also at the Epicurean and Stoic responses to his thought.

1 The quest for *eudaimonia*

In the opening of his *Nicomachean Ethics*, Aristotle (384–322 BCE) makes a basic statement upon which his ethics is to depend:

> Every craft and every investigation, and likewise every action and decision, seems to aim at some good; hence the good has been well described as that at which everything aims.

What is meant by 'good' here is a goal or purpose, something that is wanted for its own sake and not for the sake of something else. Aristotle seeks 'the good', the best of goods, and he finds it in the idea of *eudaimonia*, which is generally translated as 'happiness'. He sees happiness as the fundamental goal of life because of the way in which it relates to other goals. For whereas he sees honour, pleasure and understanding as valid goals in themselves, he thinks that people also pursue them because they believe that they will find happiness in doing so. On the other hand, he argues that nobody pursues happiness for the sake of something else.

In other words, it makes sense to say 'I want to be X in order to be happy' but nobody is going to say 'I want to be happy in order to be X'. Thus happiness is a goal that lies beneath and holds together the other valid goals that a person may choose. In itself is makes life worthwhile:

> … we regard something as self-sufficient when all by itself it makes a life choiceworthy and lacking nothing; and that is what we think happiness does.

Nicomachean Ethics, Book 1

The English word 'happiness' does not really convey what Aristotle meant by *eudaimonia*. Aristotle used it to describe a situation in which a person both experienced life as going well (our usual meaning of happiness) and also behaved well. In other words, *eudaimonia* included the idea of virtue. Now virtue is not simply a state in which one finds oneself, rather it is a disposition to act in a certain way. A person is called virtuous if, given certain circumstances, he or she can be expected to act in a way that is kindly, generous, moral, etc. One of the problems for ethics is how virtue is related to happiness. Should you strive for virtue, and believe that your happiness will follow? Why should we assume that they go together? What of the person who is virtuous but miserable? And if they do not inevitably go together, which should you aim for, virtue or happiness? We shall look at these issues a little later. For now, we need to note that Aristotle included both in his concept of *eudaimonia*.

What should be absolutely clear, however, is that when Aristotle makes 'happiness' the goal of life, he is *not* equating it with pleasure. In Section 5 of Book 1 of the *Nicomachean Ethics* he claims that there are three types of lives: of gratification, of political activity and of study. Of the first, his contempt is clear:

> The many, the most vulgar, seemingly conceive the good and happiness as pleasure, and hence they also like the life of gratification. Here they appear completely slavish, since the life they decide on is a life for grazing animals.

The second is important, for he sees Ethics in the context of the involvement in the life of the *polis* (the city state), but the last – the life of study – he regards most highly.

Notice that, when a person seeks happiness, it is something that (potentially at least) belongs to this world; it is a state that is imaginable. So Aristotle's goal is a potential situation for actual human beings. Contrast this with Plato: for Plato, the final goal was the Form of the Good – but that was not an actual state to be experienced. It was transcendent, in a world of the Forms and not in the world of particulars. One could not (to use Plato's analogy) look directly at the sun without hurting one's eyes, yet the sun was the source of light by which other things could be seen.

Aristotle disagrees with Plato's view that the Form of the Good is something eternal, of which individual good things here are mere copies. Goodness is goodness – what we see here is the real thing, not some pale reflection. He puts it this way:

> Good Itself will be no more of a good by being eternal; for a white thing is no whiter if it lasts a long time than if it lasts a day.

He can't see the point of trying to understand something that is remote from one's immediate experience:

... it is a puzzle to know what the weaver or carpenter will gain for his own craft from knowing this Good Itself, or how anyone will be better at medicine or generalship from having gazed on the Idea Itself. For what the doctor appears to consider is not even health [universally, let alone good universally], but human beings' health, and even more than that, presumably, this human being's health, since it is particular patients he treats.

a) Reason

Aristotle made the crucial distinction between form and material substance. What makes you a human being is not the individual bits of flesh and bone of which you are comprised, but the overall way in which all such material is organised into your body. But this 'form' of a human being is more than just the physical body, it is all that the person is. Aristotle said that the soul was the 'form' of the body – in other words, one's soul was the shape and meaning and purposeful direction of one's life. He then argued that the distinctive human quality was reason. It is the ability to think that sets humankind apart from all other things, and therefore reason becomes the supreme human virtue.

So reason is needed in order to be fully human. But, for Aristotle, reason was not just the faculty of thinking, which could be developed simply by being instructed in logic, but included a moral sense. In other words, human reason included the idea of obeying the precepts of reason, putting into practice what one intellectually judged to be good.

> **Note:**
> Notice here an important thread that runs from Socrates, through Plato, to Aristotle. The faculty of reason is not merely one of understanding, but also one of action: *ethics is reason put into practice*. It is very important to keep this in mind, since there are other approaches to ethics (for example, in Christian ethics, particularly as presented by Luther) in which human reason is seen as essentially 'fallen' and unable to be a valid basis for morality.

Reason, therefore, involves understanding, responding and choosing. And that is why reason is related closely to *eudaimonia*. Human excellence consists in making choices, based on practical reason, which will lead to the overall goal of humankind, which is *eudaimonia* – happiness.

For Aristotle, the unique feature of human life is reason, and therefore actions are to be judged in the light of reason. It is reason that leads people to seek their chosen end (their **telos**) and the ability to think about actions and match them up with a chosen *telos* is *phronesis* (prudence).

Morality is concerned with those actions that do, or do not, conform to the rational application of prudence to achieve a chosen end. Of all the actions that are pleasant, Aristotle sees intellectual reasoning as the highest, for it contemplates truths that are timeless. A person who is engaged in such reasoning is superior to another who is dominated by emotion, or who behaves simply out of hope of reward or the avoidance of punishment.

The ideal human *telos*, therefore, would seem to be to live the life of a Greek gentleman philosopher – Aristotle's 'great-souled man'. He is rational, balanced, good company among his equals, and above all independent. His chosen end is *eudaimonia* – to live well and to fulfil himself by behaving in a way that demonstrates the highest human quality, rationality. If he develops a friendship with someone it is for a purpose – because it is useful or pleasant – rather than being friendship for its own sake. If Plato's Form of the Good were considered a remote and other-worldly goal, then Aristotle's great-souled man is very much a worldly, self-satisfied and culturally conditioned alternative.

2 The mean

The most problematic aspect of Aristotle's ethics is his idea of **the mean**. He argued that – in the case of both emotions and actions – the difference between virtue and vice was a matter of balance or extreme. To take one of his examples, he says that jealousy is a vice because one becomes upset by the good fortune of another person, even if that good fortune is deserved. On the other hand, he considers it quite reasonable to become indignant at the good fortune of another person if that good fortune is undeserved. In other words, to be righteously indignant is fine, as long as it is held in balance. If it is taken to the extreme, it becomes jealousy and therefore a vice.

One implication of this view is that emotions and actions are morally neutral in themselves, and that it is only an extreme form of them that counts as a vice. A criticism of Aristotle on this point (for example, by Alasdair MacIntyre) is that there are some emotions, such as malice, and some actions, such as theft or murder, which are inherently evil. It is not quite that simple, however, since the term 'murder' indicates that the situation is extreme. To practise capital punishment or killing people in war would then be considered a balanced reason for carrying out the same act of taking a life. What Aristotle's theory does not in itself take into account are the circumstances in which an action is performed or emotion experienced. Thus, to use our existing example, it is these, rather than the act itself, that turn lawful killing into murder.

Perhaps it would be better to say that Aristotle's idea of the mean is such that a reasonable and appropriate action is judged a virtue and an extreme (and therefore unreasonable) one is judged a vice.

When it comes to the key area of justice, Aristotle still considers justice to be a mean, but of a rather different sort:

> ... justice is intermediate between doing injustice and suffering injustice, since doing injustice is having too much and suffering injustice is having too little.
>
> Justice is a mean, not as the other virtues are, but because it concerns an intermediate position, while injustice concerns the extremes. Justice is a virtue that the just person is said to express in the just actions expressing his decision, distributing good things and bad, both between himself and others and between others.

> *Nicomachean Ethics Book 5, Section 8*

a) Doing well and doing what is right

It is important to keep in mind the distinction, made by Alasdair MacIntyre in his text *A Short History of Ethics*, between the Greek idea of morality in terms of 'faring well' and the modern view of morality as 'doing right'. Modern ethics seeks to know what is right or wrong without linking those terms overtly to the quality of life that they offer. That is not the case with Aristotle – his ethics are aimed squarely at the good life, in which happiness and virtue, blending into a range of virtues exemplified by the life of the philosopher, are set up as the ultimate criteria by which to judge all human action.

> **Note:**
> It is important not to dismiss Aristotle's concerns for the good life as being in some way simply a matter of self-interest and therefore not 'moral'. In its modern use, 'morality' is often regarded as something that only comes into play when there is a choice between our natural inclinations (along with the prospect of 'doing well') and what we feel is our duty. Thus, being morally good is often assumed to involve some loss of well-being in favour of a higher goal. This view is particularly influenced by Protestant Christianity, with its view that human nature is 'fallen' and therefore that people's natural inclinations are bound to be wrong. It assumes that the world's natural ordering is independent of the moral stance a person takes, and that morality goes beyond practical considerations of 'faring well'. This was particularly true of Kant (see Chapter 10), who has been so influential in ethics. He saw morality as being a matter for the pure practical reason,

independent of one's experience or the expected results of an action.

Not so for the Greeks. Their concern with ethics was to see how people should live well. Hence Aristotle's placing 'happiness' as the ultimate goal. There are not two worlds here, a natural and a spiritual/moral. There is simply a single world in which people make choices that affect their happiness and that of others.

One final point we need to note about Aristotle's approach. He argued that people do not make decisions about ends but about means:

> We deliberate not about ends, but about what promotes ends; a doctor, e.g., does not deliberate about whether he will cure, or an orator about whether he will persuade, or a politician about whether he will produce good order, or any other [expert] about the end [that his science aims at].
>
> Rather, we first lay down the end, and then examine the ways and means to achieve it.
>
> … hence we deliberate about what promotes an end, not about the end.

This raises the same issue as intuitionism (see page 36), where fundamental concepts such as goodness and beauty are beyond rational debate. Aristotle seems to imply that our chosen 'end' is something that we just have in the back of our minds, informing, but not part of, the practical choices we make. It leads us to ask: Is ethics about the goals people have, or the means they employ to achieve them?

b) The context

The qualities that Aristotle judges to be virtues – courage, temperance, gentleness, liberality, wittiness, magnificence, being agreeable in company – show that the norm of behaviour that he considers is that of the free man within the upper classes of Greek society. In the end, although he does not state it in quite these blunt terms, Aristotle's ethics comes to the view that the highest good to which one can aspire is to be like … Aristotle!

In summing up the Greek contribution to ethics, Alasdair MacIntyre makes the important point that the work of Plato and Aristotle needs to be seen against the background of the decline of the *polis*. Whereas, for Plato, philosophers are rulers, they are ideal rulers who do not match up with the actual situations that he encountered. By contrast, Aristotle sees the prime function of philosophers as thinking and contemplating, rather than direct involvement in political life, and thus disengages ethics from its political matrix. His was a time (particularly under his pupil,

Alexander the Great) when the smaller city states were to give way to larger monarchies and empires. In such a situation, power and decision-making is focused in the individual monarch, and other people become citizens of the state. Thus as we move on from the time of Plato and Aristotle, we find that morality is far more concerned with the individual, and the political aspects of ethics mainly concern the relationship between the individual and the state.

3 The Epicureans

Named after Epicurus (341–270 BCE), and associated particularly with Lucretius (95–52 BCE), Epicurean philosophy took as its starting point the idea that the whole world was composed of impersonal atoms, and that everything that happened was the result of absolute physical determinism. In this they were following the earlier 'atomists', particularly Democritus. Therefore they did not see the universe as a moral place, but as entirely neutral. If people choose to behave morally, that fact does not reflect any universal structure, but is simply a choice made by humans for their own particular ends.

Like Aristotle, they saw morality implied the making of choices in order to achieve a chosen end. They saw that end as human pleasure, although they regarded the virtues as the art of achieving it. In other words, you might well restrain your inclinations, but that was only because unrestrained inclinations can lead eventually to more pain than pleasure. For example, one might feel inclined to drink alcohol, and might find that in small quantities it appears to offer pleasure, but as intake increases it leads to sickness and ultimately death. The element of prudence, restricting the appetite for more and more alcohol, is not applied because of some external moral principle preventing one from achieving pleasure, quite the reverse. The restraint is applied in order to achieve longer-term happiness.

Notice however that the basis of ethics has changed. When we looked at Plato, ethics was based very much on a person's place within the social and political life of the Greek city state. One behaved in accordance to one's place on the social scale. Then, when we came to Aristotle, the criteria became more general but also more individualistic. Qualities that make for social harmony were regarded as virtues not because they made for social harmony, but because they ultimately benefited the individual. The great-souled man is independent – or rather, if he does depend on the help of slaves to maintain his lifestyle, he does not take that into account in his moral thinking! Now with the Epicureans (and, as we shall see, with the Stoics) we find a moral theory that is related to an individual's chosen end within an impersonal and morally neutral universe. All the conventional virtues are still accepted, but they are now a means to an end – individual human happiness – rather than an end in themselves or for reasons of society.

Here ethics starts to be concerned with the individual and his or her place in the universe. How that relates to the relative place of people within society becomes a secondary matter – politics, sociology and ethics have separated themselves out.

4 The Stoics

The Stoics took a view of the universe and of ethics that was quite different from that of the Epicureans. The founder of this school of thought was Zeno (*c.*334–262 BCE) and early Stoics included Cleanthes and Chrysippus. It was a philosophy that was influential in later Roman thought, where its exponents included Seneca (1–65 CE), Epictetus (50–130 CE) and the emperor Marcus Aurelius (121–180 CE), whose *Meditations* are a good source of information about Stoic views.

The Stoics believed that the universe was ordered by divine providence, that there was a fundamental principle (the **logos**) that determined everything that happened, and that – by definition – the *logos* was good. Since everything, including one's own future welfare, was determined by a morally good agent, it made no sense to seek happiness as the goal of life. Rather, they sought to live in a way that fitted in with the overall, rational plan of the universe, and hoped that happiness might follow.

In this sense, the Stoics came closer to modern views of morality than either the Epicureans or Aristotle. They held that what counted was to make an effort to act morally, irrespective of the consequences, and to act through reason rather than through emotion. Such morality they considered to be the only 'good' and immorality the only 'evil'.

The natural ethical response to the Stoics' sense of universal order was to act with integrity, since the human soul was thought to be part of a wider world soul. Every human action is controlled by universal laws, but where we are free to make a choice we should be aware of the part we are called to play within the overall scheme of things. If you do what is right, you are at one with the basic reason that guides the whole universe. That, and that alone, is the basis of morality. Exclude any thoughts of personal gain, or the promptings of the emotions; act in tune with the universe and do what is right, leaving the final outcome to God:

> Do not seek to have events happen as you want them to, but instead want them to happen as they do happen, and your life will go well.

> *Epictetus,* Eucheiridion, Note 8

That sounds a rather negative view – hope for nothing and you will not be disappointed. But in fact, there is a good reason Epictetus takes this line:

> You are foolish if you want your children and your wife and your friends to live for ever, since you are wanting things to be up to you that are not up to you, and things to be yours that are not yours. You are stupid in the same way if you want your slave boy to be faultless, since you are wanting badness not to be badness but something else. But wanting not to fail to get what you desire – this you are capable of. A person's master is someone who has power over what he wants or does not want, either to obtain it or take it away. Whoever wants to be free, therefore, let him not want or avoid anything that is up to others. Otherwise he will necessarily be a slave.
>
> *Epictetus, Note 14 – both quotes from Cahn (ed.)*
> Classics of Western Philosophy

Therefore, key features for a Stoic approach are:

- recognise reality for what it is, and do not pretend it is different;
- take responsibility for what is up to you, not for what is not up to you;
- there is a universal order determining events;
- what matters is not the result of action (that is not up to you) but the act of will to do what is right.

Notice the important shift that has taken place. Aristotle spoke of the purpose or end (*telos*) to which every act tends. He saw happiness (*eudaimonia*) as that end for humankind. In the end a person sought what was in his or her own best interest, allowing for the fact that virtue would contribute to that 'happiness'. The Stoics went on to give a universal structure that would give virtue a value quite apart from any individual happiness that might arise because of it. For the Stoics, it was useless to build morality on possible results, because they would always be uncertain. Morality therefore had to stand on its own feet, as an end in itself, and as an expression in the individual will of the universal rational principle that orders everything.

Such Stoic attitudes, blended with the newly growing Christian religion, suggested a place for morality within the divine scheme for the universe – something we find particularly in the work of the medieval philosopher and theologian Thomas Aquinas. This approach can be termed Natural Law – in other words, that everything has an overall rational purpose within the universe, and that recognition of that purpose is a basis for moral action.

Summary List

- Aristotle argues for 'happiness' as the end or purpose of life.
- Reason is the faculty that aligns our choices to our 'happiness'.
- Virtue is a 'mean' between two extremes, each of which counts as a vice.
- The Epicureans held that everything in the universe is determined and therefore morally neutral. People are free to choose their own goal.
- The Stoics argued that the universe exhibited reason and purpose (*logos*), and that one's own good lay in aligning oneself to that universal purpose, with emphasis on the intention rather than the result of action.

Questions

1. What distinguishes the Greek term *eudaimonia* from the English word 'happiness'? Explain the significance of this for an understanding of Aristotle's ethics. Do you consider *eudaimonia* to be the good at which everyone aims? Give your reasons.
2. Explain with examples Aristotle's concept of 'the mean'. Do you consider Aristotle's idea of 'the mean' to be an adequate way of evaluating right and wrong? When would it be right not to seek a 'mean'?
3. Aristotle's ideal person would be smug. Discuss.

This essay question gives an opportunity to look at the whole background to Aristotle, and to the ideal of being a well-rounded individual. It might be questioned whether this is the sort of ethics that would make sense to a slave, for example. It extends to modern considerations of what we consider to be a moral life, and how it relates to living well.

4. Is the Stoic view that we should not be concerned about what we cannot change negative or simply realistic? Discuss.

This is quite an important issue, in terms of recognising and conforming to that which is beyond your power to change, and recognising the frustration of attempting to do otherwise.

Debate Topic

- Of all the ancient thinkers, the Epicureans would best have understood the ethical debates of the twentieth century.

With their idea of an impersonal universe and the need for humankind to construct its own goals and values, there are many parallels between the Epicureans and the logical positivist rejection of religion and morality, and the ethical responses to it.

7 Aquinas and Natural Law

KEYWORDS

efficient cause – the agent that brings something about

final cause – the final aim or purpose of something

Thomas Aquinas (1225–74) wrote from within the Christian tradition and sought to present a rational basis for Christian morality. In doing this, he was profoundly influenced by Aristotle, whose work was beginning to be examined and taught again in European universities in the thirteenth century. The result of this fusion of the secular philosophy of Aristotle and the religious tradition of the Catholic Church produced what is known as the Natural Law approach to ethics, a version of which had already been developed by the Stoics (see Chapter 6, page 59).

1 Two approaches to Christian morality

> **KEY ISSUE** Christian ethics can be divided into two very different approaches, based either on authority, or on Natural Law.

a) Authority

It is possible to see Christian ethics as arising out of principles and a spiritual situation that is in contrast to that of non-Christians. It takes the scriptures (as interpreted by the Church), the authority of Church leaders and the inspiration of the Holy Spirit as sources of authority. By contrast, it sees any system of morality based on human reason as of very limited value. This stems from the theological conviction that, since the 'Fall' in the Garden of Eden, all natural human life, including human reason, is separated from God through sin, unable to know and respond to God's Will. This view (which has developed in the main within the Protestant tradition) sees no point in trying to use human reason as the basis for ethics; rather, all Christian morality comes through the revelation of God himself. This approach was taken at the Reformation by Martin Luther, and in the twentieth century it was found in Protestant writers such as Dietrich Bonhoeffer (see his *Ethics*, 1949).

b) Natural Law

The other approach is one that we shall consider in this chapter – Natural Law. This is based on Aristotle's idea that everything has a purpose, revealed in its design (or natural 'form'), and that the fulfilment of that design is the supreme 'good' to be sought. This approach did not claim that Christian morality could be based on human reason alone, or that it could operate without any input from revelation. Rather, it argued that human reason (given by God) was a starting point for morality. Reason could offer a logical basis for those moral precepts that were also known through revelation, and which could be supplemented by the specific moral rules presented in the Scriptures.

This was seen as a particularly valuable approach where moral dilemmas occurred for which there was no biblical precedent, and for which there was therefore no obviously relevant principle given by revelation. The Natural Law approach dominates Catholic moral thinking.

2 Final causes

Aristotle makes an important distinction between an **efficient cause** and a **final cause**. An efficient cause is the agent of change that brings about its effect – in other words, it is what we would normally call a 'cause'. If we ask 'Why did the car skid off the road?', we want to know about the road surface, the state of the car's tyres and so on. In other words, we are looking for those things in existence immediately prior to whatever we are examining, which contributed to it happening. That is a question of 'efficient causes'. On the other hand, if I ask 'Why is that abstract sculpture shaped that way?', I do not look for an answer in terms of the way the sculptor angled his or her chisel, or the specific order in which material was cut away from the original block. Rather, I am interested in the concept in the sculptor's mind – the purpose and aim that explains why the sculpture is as it is. That purpose is the 'final cause' of the sculpture.

Now we can examine the whole universe in terms of 'efficient causation'. We look for the sequence of events that brings about a particular result. But that leaves out of account any sense of overall design or purpose – any 'final cause'.

The Natural Law argument depends upon this distinction. It assumes that – by whatever means employed – the world is the creation of God, and that it should therefore reveal his purpose in creating it. Natural Law is therefore based on a rational interpretation of purposiveness within the world, not simply on an objective account of what is in fact the case.

This is how Aquinas links the Aristotelian idea of agents and ends with the Christian idea of God as creating a purpose for everything:

> Now everything that is produced through the will of an agent is directed to an end by that agent: because the good and the end are the proper object of the will, wherefore whatever precedes from a will must needs be directed to an end. And each thing attains its end by its own action, which action needs to be directed by Him who endowed things with principles whereby they act.
>
> Consequently God, who in Himself is perfect in every way, and by His power endows all things with being, must needs be the Ruler of all, Himself ruled by none: nor is any thing to be excepted from His ruling, as neither is there any thing that does not owe its being to Him. Therefore as He is perfect in being and causing, so is He perfect in ruling.
>
> The effect of this ruling is seen to differ in different things, according to the difference of natures. For some things are so produced by God that, being intelligent, they bear a resemblance to Him and reflect His image: wherefore not only are they directed, but they direct themselves to their appointed end by their own actions. And if in thus directing themselves they be subject to the divine ruling, they are admitted by that divine ruling to the attainment of their last end; but are excluded therefrom if they direct themselves otherwise.
>
> Summa contra Gentiles, *Book 3, Section 1*

In other words: human beings, since they are intelligent, are able to direct themselves and therefore take responsibility for knowing and doing what God intends for them. Therefore human reason is required to examine and follow the sense of purpose that, according to Aquinas, God gives the world by virtue of being its creator.

3 Features of Natural Law

- Natural Law can refer simply to the observed laws of nature. In this sense it is simply a matter of science – which was originally called 'Natural Philosophy'. This is *not* what the Natural Law argument is based on, since it is quite possible to look at the 'efficient' causes of things without seeing any sense of 'good' or purpose or design within them.
- As presented by Aquinas, the Natural Law approach is based on the religious conviction that God created the world, establishing within it a sense of order and purpose that reflects his will.
- If everything is created for a purpose, human reason, in examining that purpose, is able to judge how to act in order to conform to that purpose.
- In the Natural Law approach to ethics, the action itself can be either natural or unnatural, and is judged on that basis. It does not depend for

its moral justification upon any results. Thus an action can be deemed morally good in itself, even if it brings about suffering.

- Since Natural Law is based on reason rather than revelation, it is in principle discoverable by anyone, whether religious or not. For the same reason, it is universal, rather than culturally conditioned.

The most obvious and widely discussed application of the Natural Law argument within the Catholic Church concerns the purpose of sex and the implications this has for contraception:

- Clearly, the 'final cause' of the sexual act is the procreation of children.
- The 'efficient cause' of the sexual act is the erotic attraction and stimulation that makes the act both desirable and possible.
- But that attraction and stimulation arises because of biological processes that have developed in order to encourage suitable breeding. The individual may not experience that sexual drive in terms of producing children, but that is its biological origin.
- Therefore, whatever the actual experience and intentions of those engaging in the act of intercourse, the 'final cause' is clearly related to conceiving children.
- The Natural Law argument therefore argues that any action taken to frustrate that natural end is morally wrong.
- This is not negated by the argument that within nature the vast majority of sperm never fertilise an egg, since each sperm is designed with the fertilisation of an egg as its goal, even if it does not actually succeed in doing so.
- Hence the Natural Law argument would see contraception, homosexuality and masturbation as inherently wrong, since they cannot lead to the 'final cause' of sexuality in conception.

The 'Natural Law' approach to ethics can claim to have an advantage over one that is based on the expected results of an action, namely that results cannot always be predicted, and can never be fully assessed. By contrast, this theory declares an act to be right or wrong quite apart from its consequences. The act can therefore be assessed morally prior to acting, and – provided that the Natural Law argument has been correctly applied – it is difficult to see how that assessment can later be overturned. It may also claim the advantage of being rationally based, and therefore not dependent upon the feelings of the person concerned. Feelings can change, but the issue of right and wrong remains fixed.

On the other hand, like many arguments, the Natural Law argument is vulnerable in terms of its presuppositions. It takes as its starting point belief in the purposive nature of the natural world. In its earlier Greek form, it saw reason (in the form of the *logos*) as an inherent feature of the universe; in its Christian form it saw the world as the product of a purposeful creator God. If, faced with the apparent meaninglessness of events on a cosmic scale, or the purposelessness of innocent suffering, one comes to the conclusion that the universe does not conform to the expectations of human reason, or that it is unlikely to be the product of an omnipotent or loving Creator, then the Natural Law argument loses its foundation.

In other words:

If we interpret the world as a place where everything has a 'final cause' or purpose,

Then we can decide what is right or wrong accordingly,

But if there is no 'final cause', there is no means of judging any one thing to be more appropriate than another.

a) Casuistry

Casuistry is the term used for the process whereby the general principles of Natural Law are applied to specific cases, and it is used generally for any system that starts with fixed principles and then applies them logically to individual situations. The word 'casuistry' tends to have a pejorative sense, in that a moral assessment based on it can depend upon the skill of the person who is arguing the case for or against. It can therefore be caricatured as insensitive and authoritarian. On the other hand, it should be recognised that any system of ethics that is going to make any claim to universal or absolute principles is going to involve some form of casuistry.

b) The Cardinal Virtues

In *Summa Theologica*, Aquinas sets out four human qualities that reflect the moral life: prudence, justice, fortitude and temperance. These are known as the **Four Cardinal Virtues** (the word 'cardinal' comes from *cardo*, meaning a hinge), and they were taken by the Stoics as the basis of the moral life. They also feature in both Plato and Aristotle. They represent the human qualities that reason suggests are required in order to live a moral life and to achieve the 'final cause' that reason sees as the overall purpose in life. The opposite of these cardinal virtues are the seven capital vices: pride, avarice, lust, envy, gluttony, anger and sloth – often referred to as the 'seven deadly sins'.

Notice that these virtues and vices, as they appear in Aquinas' writing, are based on reason and on the sense of purpose in life. They stand independent of any specifically Christian revelation. Thus, for example, the cardinal virtues might be contrasted with the theological virtues – faith, hope and love – which appear in the New Testament.

c) Theology and reason

Natural Law arguments these days are associated with Christian moral thought, particularly within the Catholic tradition. They are connected with issues of authority and with Canon Law (see page 127). On the other hand, as an argument, Natural Law is based on reason and is a development of Greek, and particularly Stoic principles.

Notice that Lutheran and other Protestant theological positions oppose Natural Law on the grounds that it gives to humankind a moral status independent of God's grace. They believe that any such status undermines the belief that salvation comes through God's grace, rather than by keeping moral rules. On the other hand, some might want to argue that the Natural Law approach is a first step – a level of morality that can be shared with those who are non-believers.

What is clear, however, is that as a theory, it depends on reason. It has become identified with Christianity simply because the reasoned argument in favour of a purposive universe is one that is now identified with belief in God, and thus the basis of religious ethics.

There is another important point to be recognised here. We saw earlier that it is basic to ethics that an 'ought' cannot be derived from an 'is' (see page 25). But clearly that is what the Natural Law argument is doing – it is setting up moral norms based on a perceived sense of purpose within the natural order. But there is one important factor to be taken into account, namely that in Natural Law the view of the universe as purposeful is not given in terms of sense experience, rather it is an *interpretation* of that experience. The fact that something has a 'final cause' or purpose is not given directly as part of the experience of that thing, rather it is the interpretation that the rational mind gives to its place in the whole scheme of things. Hence the perception of morality in Natural Law is simply the application to individual situations of that overall perception of a purposeful world.

d) The attempt to integrate perception, with its limitations

When we move on to consider other ethical theories, we shall see that some are based on expected results (utilitarianism), others on emotion (English moralism), and yet others on a radical separation of the human will or human development from any external facts about the universe (this last being a line of argument that will take us from Kant, through Nietzsche, to existentialism). In contrast to all of these, Natural Law is the attempt to use human reason to relate ethics to the general structure of the universe. The *Summa Theologica* is a drawing together of metaphysics (the branch of philosophy that considers what is real), ethics and religion. It is a monumental attempt to find a way of integrating one's whole perception of reality, humankind's place within it and the moral implications of that place. There are some fundamental problems with any Natural Law approach, however:

● How do we know what is natural? Should we judge it according to the natural outworking of physical laws? If so, should we ever try to prolong the life of someone who is ill, for death may well be the natural result of illness?

● What happens when specific religious moral injunctions conflict with the more general principles that are given by Natural Law? For example, Christ instructed his followers to turn the other cheek when abused. However, faced with someone who seeks to do you harm, Natural Law would suggest that one has a right to self-preservation.

● Finally and more generally, we need to ask if people are in fact motivated by reason. A case could be made for saying that most moral choices are made as the result of unconscious promptings that are based on needs laid down in infancy, and are not the result of any logical assessment of the 'final cause' of human life.

● Natural Law shows what our moral life should be like, on the assumption that we are rational beings and that we live in a world that has been designed by a rational and purposeful Creator. If either of these assumptions is challenged, so is the theory of Natural Law.

Summary List

● Christian morality can either contrast itself with rational morality, seeing human reason as 'fallen', or it can argue from an overall sense of purpose in the universe towards Christian moral precepts, via the concept of Natural Law.

● Natural Law is based on Aristotle's idea of the 'final cause' or purpose in everything. That which frustrates the purpose for which something has been created is deemed to be wrong.

● The cardinal virtues are qualities that reason suggests are required in order to live a moral life.

● Natural Law ethics depends on the belief that the world has been designed by a rational and purposeful Creator.

Questions

1. Explain the difference between an 'efficient' and a 'final cause'. What is the significance of this for the Natural Law approach to ethics?

2. 'Any sexual aberration which does not allow a person to find fulfilment in married love or in a balanced life of celibacy proves to be a grave encumbrance to freedom and joy, and troublesome in interpersonal relationships.' (*Medical Ethics*, Bernard Haring, 1972). This very traditional statement, from a Catholic theologian writing over 30 years ago, is critical of all forms of sexuality other than heterosexual relations between those who are married. Explain how such a view might be justified by a Natural Law argument. Do you agree with Haring's statement that other forms of sexuality are 'troublesome'? Give your reasons.

Sexuality and contraception are the most obvious areas in which a Natural Law ethic can be explored. The above quotation does not actually appeal directly to Natural Law, but raises the issue of how you understand sexuality both in terms of personal fulfilment and social conformity. Views on these will provide a useful touchstone for assessing the place of Natural Law arguments in this area.

3. Assess the strengths and weaknesses of the Natural Law view of ethics.

4. To what extent do you consider the Natural Law view of ethics to be dependent upon belief in God?

This can relate directly to the idea of God's Will being expressed through nature. You might, however, want to compare the Christian view of Natural Law with the earlier Stoic approach set out in the last chapter. The issue then becomes whether the universe is basically a rational and purposive place, or (as for the Epicureans) impersonal and dominated by chance. For students taking papers in Philosophy of Religion, this topic can be related to the Cosmological and Teleological Arguments.

8 On What Should Morality Be Based?

In Plato's *Republic*, Thrasymachus presents the idea that justice is whatever is in the interests of the stronger. He does not present this as an ideal, but simply as an observation of what actually happens in society. Plato, in the person of Socrates, finds this inadequate. But it leaves us with a fundamental question. What actually is the starting point for morality? How does it arise within a society and how is it sustained? Is it based on pure reason, or mutual agreement or emotion?

In this chapter we shall look at a number of thinkers, writing in the seventeenth and eighteenth centuries, who argued that morality is based on emotion rather than reason, but that it can be expressed and sustained by means of a contract, drawn up either between the ruler and the ruled or expressing the general will of the people, for their mutual benefit.

1 Thomas Hobbes (1588–1679)

Hobbes argued that there should be a contract between individuals and their ruler. In such a contract the ruler agrees to protect the natural rights of all the individuals who are within his jurisdiction, to act as an arbiter in disputes, and to frame laws that will enable the contract to take effect. If a ruler fails to do this, he or she has forfeited the right to govern.

Hobbes emphasises the importance of having a ruler with powers to enact the laws, otherwise he fears anarchy – a reasonable fear, given that he was writing in an England that had been torn apart by the Civil War. In return, every citizen who lives in, or passes through, the area ruled under this contract, is considered (simply by being there) to have agreed to abide by its terms. But why should such a contract for mutual security be necessary? Hobbes paints a bleak picture of a state of nature in which everyone is out for his or her own survival, a state that he sees reflected in times of war:

> Whatsoever therefore is consequent to a time of war, where every man is enemy to every man; the same is consequent to the time, wherein man lives without other security, than what their own strength, and their own invention shall furnish them withal. In such condition, there is no place for industry; because the fruit thereof is uncertain; and consequently no culture of the earth; no navigation, nor use of the commodities that may be imported by sea; no commodious building; no instruments of moving, and removing, such things as require much force; no knowledge of the face of the earth; no account of time; no arts; no letters; no society; and

which is worst of all, continual fear, and danger of violent death; and the life of man, solitary, poor, nasty, brutish, and short.

Leviathan, Ch. 6

In other words, without binding agreements, supported by force if necessary, life would descend into chaos. And clearly the main reason for accepting the authority of such a contract is fear of the anarchic alternative. This reflects the political debates of the 1640s, since *Leviathan* was published in 1651.

Hobbes argues that people should seek peace whenever possible, but if it cannot be achieved, then they have the right to go to war in order to defend themselves. This leads him to what amounts to a version of the 'golden rule':

From this fundamental law of nature, by which men are commanded to endeavour peace, is derived this second law; that a man be willing, when others are so too ... [to] be contented with so much liberty against other men, as he would allow other men against himself.

For our purpose, what we need to notice particularly here is the basis for Hobbes' contract: namely, that human nature is observed to be selfish and human action based on emotion rather than reason. People therefore need to agree together on a form of contract that will give them mutual security, and, once established, such a contract can be imposed by means of force, if necessary. Thus Hobbes sees it necessary to construct a state (his 'Leviathan') with absolute powers.

Morality is not established (as for Aristotle or Aquinas) by the appreciation of an overall sense of design and purpose, but imposed by mutual agreement in order to curb the selfishness of human emotions. We shall return to this point a little later.

2 John Locke (1632–1704)

Locke also sought to legitimise the authority of the state. In his *Treatises of Government* (1690) he presented the need for a social contract as the basis of morality and social cohesion. Like Hobbes, he starts from a state of nature, but, unlike Hobbes, he does not see this as a state of natural anarchy. Rather, he sees people as having relations with one other and making claims on one another, but needing to have some authoritative and impartial arbiter to decide between competing interests. He is concerned, for example, to establish the right to private property and to the rewards of one's labour (although accepting that servants create property for their masters). He sees the social contract as the means of establishing that authority, and it is an authority that has the tacit consent of all who live within the area of its jurisdiction (as Hobbes). His contract is agreed and justified on the basis that it offers mutual benefit.

Locke moved beyond Hobbes in one crucial respect, namely that for Hobbes the ruler is responsible for the law. Once the contract is in force, the ruler is required to enact such laws as are necessary. For Locke, the ruler is under the law, and the final authority lies not with any individual, but with the institutions of the state. Thus it was Locke rather than Hobbes who set down the principles that have led towards modern democracy.

3 Jean-Jacques Rousseau (1712–78)

Rousseau took a more positive view of the natural state. He believed that there are two primitive emotions: one is the impulse to self-preservation and the other is a general repugnance at the suffering of others. He therefore saw suffering and social inequality as the result of principles imposed by society on otherwise naturally good people and, in a famous phrase, said, 'Man was born free, and everywhere he is in chains'.

Unlike Hobbes, who saw the necessity of the imposition of law, Rousseau argues that the only authority should be 'the general will'. All citizens should freely give up their absolute liberty to do exactly as they wish, in order that everyone may enjoy a basic 'civil liberty'. But the acceptance of law is something that comes from the people, it cannot be imposed on them.

The assumption Rousseau makes here is that the interests of the individual are in line with the interests of the state as a whole, and therefore that the establishing of civil liberties will be to the individual's own benefit. Rousseau sees morality as expressed through the conscience of the individual, but it is always acted out in a social context – moral issues concern the way we treat one another, and the task of a just and moral society is to enable that natural moral sense to be exercised, without placing obstacles in its way.

Social contract ideas were also put forward by Thomas Paine (1737–1809) and John Stuart Mill (1806–73), developing the concept of the rights of the individual within a democracy and considering the competing claims of individuals and minorities within society.

The details of the work of all these thinkers is a matter of politics rather than ethics. As far as ethical theory is concerned, all we need to note is that justice and morality are regarded as enshrined within a mutual agreement, and implemented by common consent through the institutions of the state. The contract is judged according to whether or not it can deliver individual rights and freedoms, compatible with the welfare of the whole of society. For practical purposes, morality becomes a human construct, necessitated either in order to overcome natural aggression or to enhance the natural desire for co-operation.

4 Modern contract and rights-based approaches

Following Hobbes, one can see that, if a group of people gather together and decide on a contract to specify how they should treat one another and what rights are to be allowed to one another, then – once that contract is agreed – everyone should be free from the fear that his or her rights are going to be abused. Thus, even if it would be in the interests of a majority, the rights of the individual should not be set aside. This approach was taken by John Rawls (1921–2002) in his important book on political philosophy, *A Theory of Justice* (1971), where he bases his idea of justice on a social contract. The people who gather to set down the terms of that contract have to set aside all the particular features that distinguish themselves from others. In other words, they have to forget who they are. Since they do not know their place in society, Rawls argues that they will opt to support the most disadvantaged in society, since they do not know whether or not they themselves will come into that category. Thus they are able to see the justice of providing for others, without any thought that, in order to do so, they themselves might lose out. He argues that each individual should have as much liberty as is consistent with allowing a similar liberty to everyone.

In the sphere of political ethics, rights-based approaches have also been taken by Robert Nozick and Ronald Dworkin. John Mackie and others have suggested that all moral theory should be based on a concept of rights. And of course, the Universal Declaration of Human Rights is an important statement of global morality.

Contract and rights-based approaches are also important in areas of applied ethics. Medical ethics provides an example of both contract-based ethics (since there is an implied contract between doctor and patient), and also an approach in which individual patients are deemed to have rights that need to be protected.

Examples
- In many situations there is either a literal or an implied contract. If you buy goods from a shop and find they are faulty, you can expect to return them and have them replaced. This is simply because the act of buying and selling involves a contract. To sell faulty goods and then refuse to take responsibility for them is deemed a crime (because the implied contract has been broken). On the other hand, one may be asked to sign a disclaimer to the effect that the seller does not guarantee the quality of what is sold. Cheap second-hand cars, for example, are sometimes 'sold as seen', which means that the contract between buyer and seller is one that recognises the possibility that the car has faults.
- A person is deemed to have certain rights and if those rights are denied, then they can claim compensation. Thus one can argue for the right to travel freely and to hold a passport. In order to stop you travelling there has to be a good reason to withhold that right (for

example, on the grounds that you are likely to cause a disturbance at a football match abroad). People sometimes claim the right to be able to hold a parade or political rally in areas where that is likely to cause disturbance (e.g. in Northern Ireland). In such cases, respect for that right is balanced against the anticipated results of exercising it, for example, if a riot might break out.

5 Emotions?

Thomas Hobbes believed that morality was a matter of the passions:

> All voluntary motions are preceded by thought, planning out the action for a purpose. That depends on appetite or desire. Love or hate, appetites and aversions are the source of thoughts leading to voluntary actions.

And such emotions lead people to call one thing good and another bad:

> But whatsoever is the object of any man's appetite or desire, that is it which he for his part calleth *good*: and the object of his hate and aversion, *evil*; and of his contempt, *vile* and *inconsiderable*. For these words of good, evil, and contemptible, are ever used with relation to the person that useth them: there being nothing simply and absolutely so; nor any common rule of good and evil, to be taken from the nature of the objects themselves; but from the person of the man, where there is no commonwealth; or, in a commonwealth, from the person that representeth it; or from an arbitrator or judge, whom men disagreeing shall by consent set up, and make his sentence the rule thereof.
>
> Leviathan, *Ch. 6*

In other words, nothing is 'good' in itself, but is only called good because it is desired, but there may be a common agreement between people about what they will consider good – which, of course, is why Hobbes then needs to introduce the idea of a social contract.

Notice however that Hobbes, like the utilitarians, was quite prepared to accept that we act on the basis of anticipated results. As we deliberate about what to do:

> ... the appetites and aversions are raised by foresight of the good and evil consequences, and sequels of the action whereof we deliberate; the good or evil effect thereof dependeth on the foresight of a long chain of consequences of which very seldom any man is able to see to the end. But so far as a man seeth, if the good in those consequences be greater than the evil, the whole chain is that which writers call *apparent* or *seeming good*.

In other words, we act on emotion, but also seek to assess results. In the end, however, such assessment is never exhaustive, and so we settle for whatever seems to us to offer the best balance in favour of the good.

Locke argued that 'good' is whatever increases pleasure and diminishes pain, but his pupil, the third Earl of Shaftesbury (1671–1713), went on from this to say that moral judgements follow a moral sense of what is amiable, and thus are based on emotion rather than reason. This became known as the 'moral sense' basis for ethics. He argued also that a virtuous man was one who regulated his inclinations and affections in such a way as to allow them to become harmonious with the inclinations and affections of other people.

The major issue here (as with Hume later) is how moral sense is related to reason. Certainly for Locke, humankind is driven by its passions. Reason plays a secondary role in assessing what should be done, and does not initiate action. This is also Shaftesbury's position, since the pleasure we find in thinking about virtue stems from our natural altruism. Notice how the assessment of emotion is quite different in Shaftesbury and Hobbes: for the former we are naturally altruistic, for the latter, naturally selfish.

Francis Hutcheson (1694–1746) continued the 'moral sense' tradition, taking the view that there was a natural sense of benevolence, and everyone fundamentally wished for the welfare of everyone else. It was Hutcheson who first produced the idea that was to be the basis of utilitarianism:

> ... that nation is best which produces the greatest happiness for the greatest numbers, and that worst which in like manner occasions misery.
>
> An Enquiry into the Original of our Ideas of Beauty and Virtue *(1725)*

Bishop Butler (1692–1752), in his *Fifteen Sermons* (1726), put forward the view that everyone has a 'superior principle of reflection or conscience' and that this 'distinguishes between the internal principles of the heart, as well as [the] external actions'. In other words, conscience is brought to bear in trying to balance duty and happiness, although Butler is forced to admit that these two things do not always coincide. The important contribution of Butler here is the idea of a hierarchy of principles, which defines human nature and which assesses and directs the actions that we take in response to the natural promptings of our emotions.

> **Note:**
> Notice in all this how important the individual has become. With the rise of Protestantism and the Civil War, people are more aware of themselves and their inclinations, recognising the need for individuals to contract together for mutual benefit. We are entering a world where morality is linked to democracy, where enlightened self-interest determines that individuals need to accept some curbing of their natural inclinations for the common good, and (for those taking a more positive view of human nature) where the natural inclination to help those in need finds expression.

David Hume (1711–76) clarified the relationship between emotion and reason in this way – that the passions are what motivate us to act, but then reason steps in and informs the passions about their effectiveness in terms of gaining happiness from the actions that they propose.

> Reason is, and ought only to be the slave of the passions, and can never pretend to any other office than to serve and obey them.

> Treatise on Human Nature (1739–40)

In seeing morality as based on the passions, he also pointed out that you could not derive an 'ought' from an 'is' (see page 25) and thus that no amount of argument based on facts about the world would be sufficient to establish a moral law. He accepted the long-term benefit of establishing and obeying rules, because we all have needs and desires, and if those desires are served best by keeping rules, then we ought to do so. In other words, obedience is in line with self-interest.

Whereas Hume took the view that passions came before reason in determining the choices that people make, Spinoza (1632–77) took a different position. He argued that self-interest was bound to be in line with a rational consideration of a person's position, since self-preservation was the most basic need, and it is perfectly natural and logical for every creature to seek its own advantage. Any selfishness in this theory is modified by the argument that everyone should be able to seek his or her own advantage, not simply be there to satisfy one's own. Such a rational approach to self-interest leads to the idea that one should seek an equal advantage for all – a view that leads into ideas of utilitarianism, to which we now turn.

Summary List

- Morality is based on the passions or emotions.
- It is subsequently channelled by reason, either in terms of reason's ability to anticipate the result of action, or by reason's establishment of social contracts of some sort.
- The individual takes centre stage in this approach to morality. The state is there in order to further the enlightened self-interest of individuals.
- Issues of 'good' and 'bad', 'right' and 'wrong' are not related to some overall metaphysic (as we saw with Aquinas' Natural Law approach, Aristotle's final cause, or Plato's Form of the Good) but are simply the terms used for those things that are approved of or disapproved of by the emotions. If reason subsequently uses them as the basis for a social contract, or suggests what the result of an action might be, the impetus to act and the final justification of what happens seems to lie with the emotional stance of the individual.

Questions

1. Hobbes takes a negative view of humankind in its natural state, whereas Rousseau takes a positive one. Which of these do you believe to be the more realistic? How does their view of the natural state influence their ethics?

In assessing whether or not these views are realistic, you could also explore whether ethics based on a contract will achieve anything. In other words, if humankind's natural state is a destructive one, can any contractual agreement overcome it? On the other hand, if people are naturally altruistic and friendly, are such agreements necessary at all?

2. Is civil disobedience or the deliberate overthrowing of an elected government ever justified? At what point, if at all, would you consider that a government had lost its right to govern?

3. Rawls creates a hypothetical situation in which people draw up the rules for their society whilst forgetting who they are, thereby always favouring those least privileged. Do you think this is a realistic approach? To what extent are factional interests a natural and necessary part of society?

Like the previous question, Questions 2 and 3 give an opportunity to explore whether, given the chance, one would opt for a 'safe' approach and legislate to support the weak, or take the risk of promoting a more competitive society. Is enlightened self-interest the only basis on which people negotiate agreements?

4. Are people fundamentally motivated to act by their emotions and, if so, are those emotions, on balance, naturally more selfish or more altruistic?

Although couched in general terms, a question of this sort can benefit from being linked to the contrasting views of Hobbes and Rousseau. It also provides an opportunity to compare the various bases upon which ethics can be established – emotion, reason, legislative agreement, etc.

Debate Topics

- Concerning civil disobedience, and the right of people to overthrow an established government, we may ask: At what point does a government lose its right to govern?
- Are people fundamentally motivated to act by their emotions and, if so, are those emotions, on balance, more naturally selfish or more naturally altruistic?

9 Utilitarianism

KEYWORDS

utilitarianism – an ethical theory by which actions are judged according to their anticipated benefits to the people involved

rule utilitarianism – utilitarian theory that takes into account the benefits gained by obeying general rules of conduct

act utilitarianism – utilitarian theory applied to individual actions

preference utilitarianism – utilitarian theory that takes into account the preferences of all those involved in a particular course of action

consequentialism – used of any ethical theory that considers the consequences of an action. Hence, utilitarianism is one form of consequentialism.

Utilitarianism has been one of the most widespread and influential ethical theories. In its simplest form it is based on the 'Principle of Utility', which is that, in any situation where there is a moral choice, one should do that which results in the greatest happiness for the greatest number of people (a phrase apparently coined by Francis Hutcheson, see page 75). The theory of utilitarianism was set out by Jeremy Bentham and developed by J S Mill and later by Henry Sidgwick. In various forms it continues to command the attention of philosophers.

1 Jeremy Bentham (1748–1832)

Bentham was very concerned with the social conditions of his day, becoming particularly involved both with hospitals and prisons. He therefore sought a moral theory in which whatever was done in a society would be judged to be right or wrong according to whether or not it benefited a majority of its citizens. He therefore argued for the Principle of Utility, by which an action is judged good or bad according to the results that it achieves:

> By utility is meant that property of any object, whereby it tends to produce benefit, advantage, pleasure, good, or happiness (all this in the present case comes to the same thing) or (what comes again to the same thing) to prevent the happening of mischief, pain, evil, or unhappiness to the party whose interest is considered: if that party be the community in general, the happiness of the community: if a particular individual, then the happiness of that individual.

> An Introduction to the Principles of Morals and Legislation, *1789,*
> *Ch.1, Section 3*

Bentham worked on the basis that society is a collection of individuals, and that what is right for society depends on securing the happiness of those individuals. In his assessment, he wanted everyone to count equally, since he believed that everyone had an equal right to happiness, irrespective of their situation. He suggested that happiness should be measured in terms of:

● its duration;
● its intensity;
● how near, immediate and certain it is;
● how free from pain, and whether or not it is likely to lead on to further pleasure.

Each action, for Bentham, is thus good or bad according to its predicted results in generating the maximum amount of happiness, shared between the maximum number of people. His assessment was therefore essentially quantitative, and it was made on the basis of actions. Whether or not an action also conformed to a rule or law was a matter of secondary consideration – his primary interest was with the happiness generated. Bentham also took the view that acting according to this principle would itself bring about an individual's greatest happiness. The Principle of Utility could therefore be followed for the pleasure of doing so, quite apart from the benefit to others.

2 John Stuart Mill (1806–73)

There are many forms of pleasure, and not all may be considered to be of equal value. For this reason, Mill wanted to go beyond the assessment of pleasure offered by Bentham. He was quite realistic about human nature in this respect, however:

> It may be objected that many who are capable of the higher pleasures occasionally, under the influence of temptation, postpone them to the lower. But this is quite compatible with a full appreciation of the intrinsic superiority of the higher. Men often, from infirmity of character, make their election for the nearer good, though they know it to be the less valuable; and this no less when the choice is between two bodily pleasures than when it is between bodily and mental. They pursue sensual indulgences to the injury of health, though perfectly aware that health is the greater good … Capacity for the nobler feelings is in most natures a very tender plant, easily killed, not only by hostile influences, but by mere want of sustenance; and in the majority of young persons it speedily dies away if the occupations to which their position in life has devoted them, and the society into which it has thrown them, are not favourable to keeping that higher capacity in exercise. Men lose their high aspirations as they lose their intellectual tastes, because they have

not time or opportunity for indulging them; and they addict themselves to inferior pleasures, not because they deliberately prefer them, but because they are either the only ones to which they have access or the only ones which they are any longer capable of enjoying. It may be questioned whether anyone who has remained equally susceptible to both classes of pleasures ever knowingly and calmly preferred the lower, though many, in all ages, have broken down in an ineffectual attempt to combine both.

Utilitarianism, 1863, Ch. 2

A possible objection to utilitarian arguments is that, in calculating the happiness to be achieved, they do not appreciate the value of self-sacrifice, which features highly in traditional Christian morality. Mill has two things to say to counter this. The first is to link his theory with Jesus' teachings, by claiming that to love your neighbour as yourself constitutes 'the ideal perfection of utilitarian morality'. The second is to give a positive role for self-sacrifice:

The utilitarian morality does recognise in human beings the power of sacrificing their own greatest good for the good of others. It only refuses to admit that the sacrifice is itself a good. A sacrifice which does not increase or tend to increase the sum total of happiness, it considers as wasted.

Utilitarianism, 1863, Ch. 2

Mill also went beyond Bentham in proposing a positive place for rules within an overall utilitarian approach. The example he uses is of a person who tells a lie in order to get some immediate advantage. He argues that society needs the principle of truthfulness, without which nobody would ever be able to trust anybody to be telling the truth. Therefore, the rule that one should tell the truth is a general means of securing the greatest happiness for the greatest number. Breaking that rule, although it might appear to offer greater happiness in the immediate situation, will in the long run lead to less happiness.

Hence he accepts what we term **rule utilitarianism**, i.e. that a utilitarian principle can lead to the framing of general rules, which, although they may be broken in exceptional circumstances, should be taken into account in any assessment of the results of an action.

Mill gives two examples of situations where he considers that it would be right not to tell the truth:

- one should not give information to someone who is likely to use it to further an evil purpose;
- one should withhold bad news from someone who is dangerously ill, for fear of causing him or her harm.

These show that Mill is still prepared to consider individual acts as well as the rules that are thought to offer general good to society. It is also worth noting that, for Mill, the ultimate justification for moral choice, and for utilitarian and all other forms of morality, is 'the conscientious feelings of mankind'. Thus, although we appear to have in utilitarianism an almost mechanical way of gaining an objective assessment of what is right or wrong (by setting out the predicted results of an action), in the end, even the application of that principle is based on the individual conscience.

The distinction is sometimes made between *strong* rule utilitarianism and *weak* rule utilitarianism, the former holding that one should never break a rule that is established on utilitarian principles, the latter that there may be situations when the likely outcome of a particular act may take precedence over the general rule in a utilitarian assessment, although of course that rule still needs to be taken into account. Some modern approaches to **act utilitarianism** tend to say that an act should be considered good if, on balance, it produces enough happiness. It is not necessary to show that it produced the maximum happiness possible. This is part of a general attempt to make utilitarian theories workable in practice, without making demands (either in terms of assessing all the possible future consequences of an action, or checking the consequences of each alternative course of action) that are impossible to satisfy.

3 Preference and motive utilitarianism

So far, in considering Bentham and Mill, we have examined act and rule utilitarianism, but alongside the assessment of those acts and rules that are deemed overall to benefit society, there are other factors that may be taken into account in a utilitarian assessment: the preferences of those involved, and the motive for acting in a particular way.

In his book *The Language of Morals* (1952), R M Hare not only set out the basis of a prescriptivist approach to moral language (see page 38) but also argued for what may be termed **preference utilitarianism**. In this, the utilitarian assessment of a situation takes into account the preferences of the individuals involved, except where those preferences come into direct conflict with the preferences of others. So the right thing to do in any situation is to maximise the satisfaction of the preferences of all those involved. This gets round the problem of using utilitarianism to impose one idea of happiness on someone who might have a very different one. On the other hand, what I prefer to do may not coincide with what is in my own interest. Hence, it may be necessary to distinguish between 'preference utilitarianism' and 'interest utilitarianism'.

There has always been a problem for utilitarianism in terms of an assessment of the motive a person may have for carrying out an action. Can something be right on utilitarian principles even if the motive for doing it is wrong? This question was addressed by Henry Sidgwick (1838–1900), who took the view that an *outcome* in terms of happiness need not be the same thing that actually *motivates* an action:

> ... the doctrine that Universal Happiness is the ultimate *standard* must not be understood to imply that Universal Benevolence is the only right or always the best *motive* of action.

And he argues that if:

> ... general happiness will be more satisfactorily attained if men frequently act from other motives than pure universal philanthropy, it is obvious that these other motives are reasonably to be preferred on Utilitarian principles.

> The Methods of Ethics, 1874

But if the motive is secondary to the actual result of the action, it is nevertheless possible to consider applying the principle of utility to motives themselves. Bentham held that a person's motive on any given occasion may be judged better or worse depending on the utility of having that motive on that occasion. In other words, the motive itself is considered good if, as a result of having it, happiness is to be increased. (But that does not seem to imply – as Sidgwick later pointed out – that the motive itself has to be the desire for the greatest happiness of the greatest number.) A modern review of motive utilitarianism is given by Robert Adams in *Utilitarianism and Its Critics* (1990).

4 Utilitarianism in practice

Take the example of a doctor who is called to the scene of an accident and is required to set a broken bone and perform other emergency procedures. His action is almost certain to cause additional pain to the person injured. Is that pain good or bad? The answer here seems clear enough, since short-term pain is outweighed by the long-term good of having limbs that grow straight. If you cause pain in the process of saving a life, there seems to be no doubt that, based on a utilitarian assessment of results, that action can be judged good.

Similarly, given the possibility of sharing happiness widely or offering it to a minority at the expense of a majority, it seems fairly clear (and certainly would have been so to those who sought social reform in the seventeenth and eighteenth centuries) that the former is the 'right' thing to do.

On the other hand, in using this argument, we need a fairly clear idea of what constitutes 'happiness'. In other words, because it is put into practice, utilitarianism requires:

- some overall set of values by which to assess happiness;
- the ability to predict which course of action is most likely to secure that happiness.

And, of course, such a prediction is always going to be provisional. It is always possible to revise one's estimate of long-term harm or benefit.

Utilitarian considerations are applied to a wide range of problems within applied ethics. Medical experimentation, whether on animals or humans, for example, is justified in terms of the anticipated benefit to other people that may result from an advance in knowledge. In environmental debates, whether it is the preservation of the environment or the protecting of rare species, the argument often used is utilitarian – that everyone will benefit in the long run from some restraint or intervention.

In the practical application of utilitarianism, it is crucial to be aware of the presuppositions of those who assess what may be considered the 'happiness' that is to be maximised, and where this is lacking, utilitarian arguments on their own are not persuasive. It may be true that, by taking a certain course of action, more people will live longer. But does that constitute the greatest happiness to the greatest number? There are many other factors to be considered.

5 Criticisms of utilitarianism

One can argue that the concept of happiness is so broad that it can be taken as the name for whatever a person takes as his or her personal goal. If that were to be the case, then, from the standpoint of the agent, utilitarianism offers no objective method of assessing the rights or wrongs of an action. Other people, with other concepts of happiness, will come to a different assessment. In such a situation, without an agreed definition of what constitutes happiness, nothing much has been achieved.

One could go on to say that happiness depends on a framework of values, and therefore that utilitarianism does not provide an independent moral theory, but a mechanical way of assessing the likelihood of achieving already stated personal and moral goals. In the end, utilitarianism must rest on something else.

Example
Imagine a society of sadists applying utilitarian principles to their particular form of pleasure. Inflicting pain would be justified in terms of the resulting happiness. If you then step outside that society and say (taking a strong rule utilitarian approach) that inflicting pain is wrong because, in the world at large, it causes suffering rather than happiness, the weak rule utilitarian will object that, in this particular

situation, the immediate satisfaction obtained takes precedence over a rule that does not hold for the people concerned. The preference utilitarian will also claim that the sadistic preferences of the agents should be taken into account. In the end, what you seem to have is a form of 'social contract' based on the passions, but not an independent or objective way of determining whether sadism is right or wrong.

The validity of using the mechanism of utilitarianism seems obvious in some cases, but not in others. Take the example of the availability of expensive medical treatment in a situation where funding is limited. For the price of one major operation, many other people's lives could be benefited or even saved by more cost-effective remedies. Does that mean that it would be wrong to operate? Or consider the situation where, as a result of the plight of an individual becoming known, many people generously contribute funds to enable that person to have specialist treatment. On a utilitarian assessment that is still a good thing, since the many who contribute do so voluntarily and therefore gain happiness in doing so.

But notice how curious this conclusion is, for the same thing can be considered wrong if imposed on people (forcing everyone to contribute for the benefit of an individual) but right if done voluntarily. This does not sound much like an objective way of assessing right and wrong, merely a way of assessing its social acceptability – which is why Hare and others have sought to take into account both preferences and motives.

Not all are satisfied with a broadly utilitarian approach to medical issues. In her book *The Elimination of Morality* (1993), Anne Maclean criticises Peter Singer and others for what she sees as the removal of all moral concepts that cannot be justified on strictly utilitarian terms. Indeed, she is critical of the whole area of philosophy and bioethics. She does not want to deny that there can be rational answers to moral questions, but she opposes the idea that 'for any moral question, there is a *uniquely* rational answer to it which can be uncovered by philosophical enquiry' (*op cit.* page 5).

This highlights a practical problem with the application of utilitarian arguments, namely that, having established a criterion for the future benefit of those involved (e.g. maximising life), that criterion can then be applied mechanically to a range of issues (e.g. the allocation of limited medical resources).

Utilitarianism depends on our ability to know what gives other people happiness, or what is for their general welfare. That is not always the case, and may change from time to time. Also, utilitarianism does not seem to account for those situations where a person feels that there is something they should do, irrespective of the consequences. It was pointed out above that Mill accepted the notion of self-sacrifice, but that he considered it wasted unless the sum of human happiness was increased as a result.

What of situations where a person dies in a failed attempt to save the life of another? According to Mill's argument, that act of self-sacrifice is wasted, since as a result of it two people are dead rather than one. But is there not a sense that the act of trying to save the life of another human being, however unlikely it is to succeed, is in some way inherently good? This is not to say that a utilitarian could find no way of justifying such an action – it could, for example, be an inspiration to many others. But it seems curious that the inherent value of that action depends on such results. *And here we touch on a central feature of utilitarianism – that goodness does not inhere in an action, but is only given by setting that action in the context of the greatest happiness of the greatest number.*

One of the most succinct and pertinent challenges to the utilitarianism of Mill was presented by G E Moore in his *Principia Ethica* (1903). In that book he is concerned to refute the naturalistic fallacy – namely the attempt to derive an 'ought' from an 'is'. He sees this as a feature of almost all previous moral systems (only Plato and Sidgwick escape his criticism). His criticism is based on his claim that Mill identifies 'good' with 'desirable':

> The fact is that 'desirable' does not mean 'able to be desired' as 'visible' means 'able to be seen'. The desirable means simply what *ought* to be desired or *deserves* to be desired ... 'Desirable' does indeed mean 'what it is good to desire'; but when this is understood, it is no longer plausible to say that our only test of that, is what is actually desired. Is it merely a tautology when the Prayer Book talks of *good* desires? Are not *bad* desires also possible?

In other words, Moore accuses Mill of slipping in an 'ought' where he should be speaking about what 'is' as a matter of fact, desired. Notice that this criticism could apply equally to Bentham, who opens his exposition of utilitarianism by saying that the sovereign powers of pain and pleasure should determine what we ought to do, as well as what we in fact do.

Bernard Williams (see 'A Critique of Utilitarianism' in *Utilitarianism: For and Against*, 1973) has argued that a person's moral identity is rooted in his or her personal commitments. In other words, the basis of morality is in personal values and projects – these constitute what a person stands for, and given a situation of moral choice, they are the things likely to decide what action should be taken.

By contrast, utilitarianism, because it requires an 'objective' assessment of results in order to justify a moral decision, requires a person to set aside personal values and commitments, and start again with each new decision. Williams wants to reinstate a place for personal integrity, which – on purely utilitarian terms – is 'more or less unintelligible' (*ibid.*). In practice, one therefore has to ask if a commitment-less approach is realistic, or indeed if it is the way in which people actually make moral decisions. *Williams has argued that we therefore need a more agent-centred approach.*

Another line of criticism, presented by John Rawls, is that utilitarianism does not take seriously the distinction between persons. This approach considers that utilitarian arguments can too easily be used to justify an impersonal approach, so that the rights of individuals are set aside for some greater good. It would also justify a paternalistic approach whereby the state could decide that your own happiness could be enhanced by measures that you personally would not wish to accept. Like Bernard Williams' approach, the key feature is recognition of individuals and their rights, integrity, preferences and personal projects. These things, it is argued, show the inadequacy of any moral system that is based on some general or impersonal assessment.

A more general problem with any form of utilitarianism is the inability ever to achieve a definite assessment of the total of happiness or suffering achieved by any action. This problem had been anticipated by Hume. *The effects of an action form part of a chain that stretches into an indefinite future. There is always the possibility that a very positive result of an action may subsequently lead to very negative consequences.*

Summary List

- Bentham and Mill both accept the Principle of Utility and the assessment of resulting happiness as the criteria for assessing the moral value of an action.
- But Mill rejected Bentham's way of assessing pleasure, being more concerned with the quality rather than quantity of happiness achieved.
- In general also, Bentham presents what is known as act utilitarianism, where the anticipated results of each individual act are taken into account, whilst Mill takes a rule utilitarian view, namely that one should obey a rule if that rule will itself bring about more happiness within society.
- Benefits of utilitarianism include its simplicity, and the way in which all considerations are brought under a single principle. It is also, as Sidgwick said, a common-sense approach.
- Criticisms include the problem of moving from an 'is' to an 'ought', the impersonal assessment of what is in other people's interest and the inadequate treatment of issues of individual rights and integrity.

Questions

1. **a)** Choose a moral issue (e.g. capital punishment; the lowering of the age of consent for homosexuals; sex outside marriage) and show how you would approach it from the standpoints of act utilitarianism, rule utilitarianism and preference utilitarianism. Then say which of these you find most helpful as a basis for an ethical argument, giving your reasons.

   or b) What are the essential differences between act, rule and preference utilitarianism? Assess the advantages and disadvantages of each.

2. Can self-sacrifice ever be good? Discuss with reference to utilitarian views of morality.

3. If utilitarianism depends on assessing the final results of an action, can we ever say for certain that something is good or bad?

4. Do personal commitments take priority over the assessment of the anticipated results of action? Discuss with reference to utilitarianism and Bernard Williams' view of moral action.

In all these questions on utilitarianism, it is valuable to be able to give examples of the problem of assessing results in dealing with moral issues. Medical ethics provides a whole range of problems of this sort, especially in terms of the allocation of medical resources. Similarly, there are many issues connected with the environment. Since utilitarianism is so widespread, and so often regarded as the common-sense approach, it is important to be able to explore the different ways in which it may be presented (act, rule and preference), and also to take a reasoned and critical approach to what it can achieve.

Discussion Topics

● Does utilitarianism offer values, or merely a mechanism for applying values we already hold?

● Is utilitarianism consistent with the ethics of a religion you have studied?

10 Kant and Moral Choice

Aquinas' sense of Natural Law, the utilitarians' weighing of the expected results of an action, and considering the obligations of an implied contract and agreement made between people: all attempted to establish some objective basis for moral claims. Immanuel Kant (1724–1804) started from a totally different position. He argued that we all know what it is to have a sense of moral obligation – to believe that there is something we *ought* to do, irrespective of the consequences it may have for us. Starting from that experience of morality, he believed that it should be possible to give a systematic account of our moral duties and of the principles upon which they are founded, which would be based on pure reason, and would therefore be universal.

1 A sense of moral obligation

KEY ISSUE For Kant, the key issue is how to discover a rational basis for one's sense of duty, and from that to devise a principle by which one could distinguish between right and wrong.

Kant's moral philosophy is a reflection upon the direct experience of morality:

> Two things fill the mind with ever new and increasing admiration and awe the oftener and more steadily we reflect on them: the starry heavens above me and the moral law within me. I do not merely conjecture them and see them as though obscured in darkness or in the transcendent region beyond my horizon: I see them before me, and I associate them directly with the consciousness of my own existence.

Critique of Practical Reason, 1788

In his *Critique of Pure Reason,* Kant had examined the traditional arguments for the existence of God and found them wanting. He had also come to the conclusion that our understanding of the world depends to a large extent upon our own faculties. Space, time and causality are not 'out there' to be discovered, but are ways in which our minds order their experience. These ideas, taken together, had a radical impact on his subsequent thinking. In a universe that lacked theological certainty, and in which – looking up at 'the starry heavens' – he was all too aware of human insignificance, he hoped that reason and the experience of morality would restore a sense of human dignity and worth. His moral theory therefore starts with the phenomenon of 'good will' and celebrates what can be achieved by the application of human reason.

He did not look at the world and ask if freedom and moral choice were possible. Instead, he started with the experience of moral choice, and then sought to find its implications. So, for example, we know we are free because we experience moral choice; we do not experience moral choice only after coming to the conclusion that we are free.

Kant saw clearly that, where empirical evidence was concerned, there could be no certainty. He also realised (from reading Hume, see page 76) that one could never argue logically from an 'is' to an 'ought', for facts show what is, not what ought to be. He therefore wanted to find a new starting point for morality, one that was not dependent on anything as ambiguous as evidence. He found it in the idea of a 'good will'.

2 The 'Good Will'

There is no possibility of thinking of anything at all in the world, or even out of it, which can be regarded as good without qualification, except a *good will.* Intelligence, wit, judgement, and whatever talents of the mind one might want to name are doubtless in many respects good and desirable, as are such qualities of temperament as courage, resolution, perseverance. But they can also become extremely bad and harmful if the will, which is to make use of these gifts of nature and which in its special constitution is called character, is not good. The same holds with gifts of fortune; power, riches, honour, even health, and that complete well-being and contentment with one's condition which is called happiness make for pride and often hereby even arrogance, unless there is a good will to correct their influence on the mind and herewith also to rectify the whole principle of action and make it universally conformable to its end. The sight of a being who is not graced by any touch of a pure and good will but who yet enjoys an uninterrupted prosperity can never delight a rational and impartial spectator. Thus a good will seems to constitute the indispensable condition of being even worthy of happiness.

Groundwork for the Metaphysics of Morals, *1785*

So we have here Kant's agenda: he wanted to place the 'good will' at the very centre of ethics, and in doing so, he was to go beyond anything that had been written before. In many ways, Kant represents a turning point in ethics – after his work, it became impossible to ignore the active role of the person who behaves morally; morality is not to be found in evidence we can analyse, nor in results we may try to predict, but only in the exercise of freedom and good will in an action.

a) The will and virtue

The second part of Kant's *The Metaphysics of Morals* concerns 'The Doctrine of Virtue'. He follows Aristotle in seeing virtue as a human excellence. What counts, if a person is to do his or her duty, is not mere obedience, but a good will. In choosing to act morally, I am exercising an inner freedom in following a sense of my purpose and destiny, and expressing my will and virtues in an exercise of pure practical reason.

Kant sees the development of virtues as its own reward, and ethics – action springing from the pure practical reason – as the sole means of bringing this about. The intention of his morality is to set aside all egocentricity, and move towards an unconditional and universal sympathy.

Note:
Notice just how different this is from the Greek and medieval thinkers we have already examined. It had earlier been assumed that 'good' could be defined with reference to the world, and therefore it was something to be discovered and explored, and in line with which one should direct one's action. This is certainly the case, for example, with Aquinas' view of Natural Law. It is good for everything to follow its natural purpose and end – doing so constitutes its 'good'. But for Kant, 'good' is related to the will, not in a set of values to be found in the world.

The implication here is that each individual constructs and takes responsibility for his or her own set of moral values.

Although he acknowledges evil, Kant does not see it as a separate power influencing one's choices or frustrating the working out of the good. Rather, he sees it as a muting of, or failure to acknowledge and respond to, the moral law. Due to our conditioning or circumstances we may be dominated by our egos, and this means that our moral choices will fail the test of the categorical imperative (see page 96), since they will be based on self-interest.

b) The *summmum bonum*

For Kant the aim of morality is not to gain happiness, but to be *worthy* of happiness. Indeed, he rather despises the person who gains happiness and fortune in life without deserving it. He sees the 'highest good' (*summum bonum*) as the joining of virtue and happiness. But it is virtue, in doing one's duty, that comes first; happiness is always a bonus that may be added, and it cannot be guaranteed. As we shall see later (page 95), this relates closely to his idea of the 'postulates' of the practical reason.

3 The background to Kant's moral theory

To appreciate Kant's ethical argument, we need to look at it in the context of his philosophy as a whole, and in particular the influences upon him.

Kant was influenced by science and by the gathering and assessment of empirical evidence. Indeed, the impetus behind his 'Copernican revolution' was the attempt to reconcile the ambiguity in empirical evidence (nothing is absolutely certain, we have only degrees of probability) that he found in Hume, with the laws of nature as framed by Newton. How can we achieve certainty from evidence alone? His answer, of course, was that we cannot: certainty comes from the mind, in actively ordering the evidence of the senses. The world is a rational place, organised in time, space and causality, not because we have sufficient evidence to convince us of that fact, but because it is our minds that perceive it that way. So much for his wondering about the starry heavens, but when it came to the experience of the moral law within him, Kant needed to take an equally bold step.

He was concerned by Hume's argument that one cannot rationally move from an 'is' to an 'ought' (in his *Treatise on Human Nature*, 1738, see page 76). From it, he concluded that morality cannot be based on the evidence of the senses. He was also convinced, however, that people had an inherent sense of right and wrong, and was influenced by Rousseau's positive view of human nature (see page 72). His task, therefore, was to reconcile the experience of moral obligation with empirical scepticism.

Note: the synthetic 'a priori'
Statements are either *a priori* (prior to experience) or *a posteriori* (after and based on experience). Kant also distinguished between 'analytic statements' (like tautologies, or mathematics, where their truth is known by definition) and 'synthetic statements', which are known to be true with reference to empirical evidence.

His response to empirical scepticism was therefore to suggest that moral statements were synthetic a priori. In other words, they did not depend on sense experience, but they had a meaning which was not limited to a definition of terms, and which could therefore be denied without logical contradiction.

a) Motives

If you are to consider the pure practical reason, you need to eliminate three other reasons why a person might choose to do something.

- You might do something because you will immediately or eventually benefit from it. In other words, you might act out of enlightened self-interest – even when you appear to be doing something to your own cost. For example, a shopkeeper may reduce the price of his goods, or offer some special deal for regular customers. On the face of it he is thereby limiting his profit and so appears to be offering something for the benefit of others. On the other hand, it is clear that a person will do that for sound commercial reasons. The customer is being offered something in order that, in the longer term, the shopkeeper may benefit. Kant would hold that such a decision cannot be given moral approval, since it is based on anticipated results, not on pure reason.
- Equally you may do something out of natural interest. Suppose I am fascinated by anatomy. I might offer to help with some major surgical operation. I may indeed make a difference and help the patient recover. Nevertheless, the impetus behind my offer of help is purely selfish. I am doing something that I enjoy, not something that I feel I have a duty to do. Kant was even against making sympathy a basis for moral action (as Hume had argued), since it is possible that we may offer sympathy to someone who does not deserve it.
- It is equally possible to do something simply because someone in authority – either a representative of the law, or of a religion, or some other person in a position of responsibility – may tell you to do it. I want to remain on good terms with that person for a whole variety of reasons, and so I decide to obey. But obedience too, although it may be considered to be a virtue (expressing loyalty), is not exactly the same as making a free moral choice.

Kant eliminates these alternative reasons and then looks to see what is left. What motivates moral action that is neither commanded, nor promises rewards nor is inherently pleasurable? *For Kant, the highest form of morality is to do one's duty against one's own inclinations.* In his *Groundwork of the Metaphysics of Morals* he set out three propositions that fix the boundaries of morality:

- your action is moral only if you act from a sense of duty;
- your action is moral only if you act on the basis of a principle, or maxim;
- it is your duty to act out of reverence for the moral law.

IMMANUEL KANT (1724–1804) -*Profile*-

Kant was born, spent his whole life and died in Königsberg in East Prussia. His most important works were the *Critique of Pure Reason* (1781), the *Groundwork of the Metaphysics of Morals* (1785), the *Critique of Practical Reason* (1788), the *Critique of Judgement* (1790), *Religion within the Limits of Reason Alone* (1793), *Eternal Peace* (1795) and *The Metaphysics of Morals* (1797).

Basically, Kant stands as part of the European Enlightenment, the attempt to get beyond authority and superstition and deal with the world on the basis of human reason. An early work, *The General History of Nature and Theory of the Heavens* (1755) was an attempt to use Newton's physical laws to explain the universe in a mechanistic way without the need for Newton's idea of an external creator God (deism). He had been influenced by German pietism, which emphasised that religion should be based on personal experience, rather than on study or rational proof. Disturbed by Hume's scepticism about what we could know as a result of sense experience, his own approach was to start with pure reason. What do we know of ourselves as rational beings?

The result, which was expounded in the *Critique of Pure Reason*, was what he was to call his Copernican revolution. It had been assumed that sense experience conformed to external reality, but – just as Copernicus had found that his observations made sense once he had realised that the Earth moved round the Sun rather than the other way round – he argued that we experience the world as we do simply because that is the way our senses function. We do not know things as they are in themselves, but only as they appear to us. Space, time and causality are not 'out there' to be discovered, but are ways in which we organise our experience.

The religious implications of his views were controversial. Following the publication of *Religion Within the Limits of Reason Alone*, he was forbidden by the university to write any more on matters of religion.

> **A killjoy?**
>
> Kant does seem something of a killjoy, since he appears to dismiss the idea that actions that we find naturally interesting, or to our benefit, or prompted by sympathy or affection, can be moral. But that is not actually fair to him. He admitted that inclination could still be present (we may, for example, simply enjoy doing our duty) but argued that our inclinations are irrelevant in considering the *moral status* of our action. In other words, if you enjoy doing something, fine, but don't try to claim that you are being virtuous.

4 The Postulates: Freedom, God and Immortality

Kant argued that, in obeying a moral command, we are accepting three things:

- Freedom: because I experience myself as having a free choice. If it wasn't possible for me to do something, I wouldn't have a sense that I ought to do it.
- God: because if I feel obliged to do something, I must have a sense that the world is designed in such a way that doing the right thing will eventually lead to happiness. In a godless world, nothing would matter.
- Immortality: because I may not be able to achieve the good I seek in following this moral obligation in the course of this lifetime. On the other hand, if I still go ahead and do it, it shows that I am in some way looking beyond this life.

Notice that Kant did not mean that we are first convinced of these three things, and then come to the conclusion that it is reasonable therefore to obey a moral command. Rather, that these three things are 'postulates' of the pure practical reason. They are implied in your sense of moral obligation.

In his *Critique of Pure Reason* (1781), Kant distinguished between things as we experience them (**phenomena**) and things as they are in themselves (**noumena**). In the world of *phenomena*, everything is totally determined, simply because our minds seek reasons for everything that happens. We impose causality upon our experience – it is the only way in which we can make sense of it. So if I look at myself from the outside, as it were, if I turn myself into a *phenomenon*, I shall be totally conditioned. Freedom will vanish, because an omniscient observer would always be able to give reasons why I acted as I did. But Kant holds that we can be both phenomenally conditioned and noumenally free. As I am in myself, I am free. As I am observed from the outside, I am conditioned.

What Kant is arguing for in the *Critique of Practical Reason* (1788) is the very opposite of what we normally assume in terms of freedom and morality. We would normally examine whether or not we are free, because if we are not then morality makes no sense, since we cannot be praised or blamed for what is beyond our control (see the general comments on freedom and determinism on pages 16–24). Kant, by contrast, points out that the reverse is the case – that it is the experience of the moral law that leads to an awareness of freedom. I only experience freedom when I reflect on the ability I have to make a moral choice.

Thus the immediate awareness of being human entails an awareness of one's own freedom and of the challenge of embodying such freedom in chosen action. Kant's basis for morality is found within our own experience of it.

Therefore, according to Kant, one should act *as if* there were a God, even if God cannot be proved. One acts to fulfil one's own moral imperative as though God had commanded it, without attachment to the results of action. But the key feature to notice here is that *acting morally has become an end in itself*. If a person believes in God, behaving morally could be seen as a way to achieve happiness by gaining His approval. However, Kant wants moral development to be free from all considerations of consequences.

a) Thinking freedom

We can look at this experience another way. In general, we think of ourselves as individual egos, separated from one another and from the rest of the world. But as soon as I think of myself in this way, I become part of the phenomenal world; I am an object among other objects, and as such I lose my freedom to act morally, because everything I do is conditioned by what is outside me.

But what if I let go of the ego, and thereby drop the distinction between the self and the world? What if I act in a way that is based on pure practical reason, not looking at the possible results of my action? I would be spontaneous, acting solely on the basis of my will, and I would therefore be free.

5 The categorical imperative

KEY ISSUES We need to distinguish between a **categorical imperative** and a **hypothetical imperative**. A hypothetical imperative tells you what you should do in order to achieve a given result (e.g. if you want to win a race, you will need to train). On the other hand, if you are not interested in the promised result, there is no need to obey the command. All hypothetical imperatives come in the form of an 'if … then' statement. By contrast a categorical imperative tells you that you should do something, without any reference to the likely result (e.g. you should always tell the truth).

Kant's theory of ethics was developed initially in *Groundwork of the Metaphysics of Morals* (1785) and in the *Critique of Practical Reason* (1788). When reflecting on the experience of moral obligation, he found that morality implied a categorical imperative. He saw nothing moral in simply following a line of action in order to achieve a desired result. He therefore sought to formulate general rules for testing whether something was right or wrong. There are three main forms of the categorical imperative, with several different forms of wording, but the first and most basic one is:

> So act that the maxim of your will could always hold at the same time as a principle establishing universal law.

A Maxim?

A maxim is a principle, or a general rule governing the action of a rational person. It takes the form, 'Whenever A happens, I consider it right to do B'. Maxims are crucial in Kant's moral theory, because they show the basis upon which the good will is operating.

This form of the categorical imperative therefore provides a simple, logical test. If you are content that everyone else should be bound by the same principle upon which you are acting, then what you are doing is logically consistent and therefore right. If, on the other hand, what you want to do would involve a contradiction, or be self-defeating, if everyone followed that same maxim, then it is wrong.

Example

Kant illustrated this by considering the situation of someone who needs a loan, and will only get it if he promises to repay it. If he knows that he will not be able to repay it, should he still go ahead and make that promise? Kant argues that it would only be right to make that promise if you could, at the same time, agree that making such a promise (i.e. one you cannot keep) should be made a universal law. But this would involve a contradiction, because promise-making becomes nonsense if everyone is entitled to break their promises. Thus, he reasons, it is always wrong to make a promise that you know you cannot keep.

Notice that the categorical imperative does not tell you the *content* of your moral obligations. *What it offers is a principle of the pure practical reason – the most general principle possible, namely that something is right only if you can, without contradiction, wish it to become a universal law.*

The second formulation of his categorical imperative concerns the treatment of other people:

Act in such a way that you always treat humanity, whether in your own person or in the person of any other, never simply as a means, but always at the same time as an end.

Notice therefore that Kant's morality is *a priori*. It is established quite apart from a consideration of possible results. In other words, he wants the motive for action to be other than the satisfaction of our immediate sensual desires. This is the very opposite of any form of hedonism or utilitarianism, where the production of happiness is the ground for choice.

Kant firmly believed that a person experienced his or her own worth primarily when acting in this way, based on *a priori* reason, and not simply responding to sense experience. Kant's moral vision here is that a person should set aside all narrow considerations of personal gain and have a genuinely universal sympathy. His argument is that, in doing so, one achieves what is highest in human nature.

The third form of the categorical imperative highlights Kant's view that it is human reason that determines morality:

Act as if [you are] a legislating member in the universal kingdom of ends.

By the 'kingdom of ends', Kant means the society of rational beings, each of whom are to be treated as 'ends' rather than as 'means'. We are to be members in such a kingdom and also its legislators. *As free, autonomous, rational, moral agents, we do not discover morality – we make it.*

a) A 'selfish' problem

Kant was trying to express the logical argument that would be presented by someone who was not concerned with his or her own ego, but was genuinely universal in his or her sympathies. To set aside personal consideration is to think universally, and it is therefore reasonable that the maxims of your actions should also be universal. The danger with his formulation is that one might use it simply as a basis for calculation from a selfish point of view. For example, I could say that it is wrong to steal, on the grounds that if everyone stole, private property would be in peril and I would have little hope of retaining what I had just stolen. That would be a straight application of the categorical imperative. But I could go on to say that it is wrong to steal except when a person is starving, since I could imagine wanting everyone to be able to steal simply in order to survive – and therefore (since I am starving) it is right for me to steal.

This is an obvious example, but there could be more subtle ones in which the maxim that is to be universalised is so closely defined that it would apply to a very limited number of people, and therefore there would be no contradiction in willing that it should become a universal law. In other words, it would be easy to argue that everyone in *exactly* the same situation as me should be able to do what I now choose to do, even if everyone in slightly different circumstances is precluded from doing so. Although that is possible, given the logic of Kant's application of the categorical imperative, it is totally against his intention in formulating it – for he wanted to get away from any calculations based on anticipated advantage for the individual or group. He considered the principle of universalisability to be necessary for an action to be considered right – if it cannot be universalised, it cannot be right.

b) The problem of others

Kant's moral theory examines what it means to be a free, autonomous, moral legislator. However, in any actual society (as opposed to the ideal 'kingdom of ends') we need to frame moral principles that restrain people from behaving in a way that is destructive to society as a whole. In other words, there will be many practical situations in which we cannot consider everyone as a morally responsible, free and autonomous 'end'. This challenge was raised by Christine Korsgaard in an article in 1986, which is reproduced in the Sterba anthology (see Further Reading).

Kant held that everything either has a price or dignity. If it has a price, it can be exchanged and replaced by something equivalent. But every human being, as an 'end', is unique and irreplaceable, and therefore has dignity. The problem is how to deal with those who choose to treat other people as though they had a price – to treat them as commodities.

Another problem, raised by Alasdair MacIntyre in *After Virtue*, is that Kant's system works on the assumption that everyone is agreed on the final end and purpose of human life. In reality, there is no such agreement. He might want everyone to be free and autonomous; others might not.

6 Absolute or relative?

Moral choices can be related to society and particularly to the established values of the society within which they are made. All ethical theories based on contract, for example, carry with them the values of those who enter into that contract. (Axiological ethics is the term sometimes used for the study of the values that underlie the moral choices people make.)

A key question for ethics is therefore whether all moral issues are culturally conditioned and actions judged right or wrong with reference to underlying values or society, or whether there is some way of getting beneath the cultural diversity and touching some absolute moral standard. It is this, of course, that Kant has attempted to do with the concept of the categorical imperative. It focuses on the sense of moral obligation without reference to the consequences of an action nor yet to the social or cultural matrix of values within which it is experienced.

Just as within his theory of knowledge, Kant saw the mind as having an active role, determining how we are to understand sense perceptions, so in the area of morality the mind is active in pursuit of its highest goals, and only in the light of these does it evaluate sense perceptions in terms of the expected results of action.

In the end, Kant's ethical theory comes down to individual integrity. What counts morally is that you should be able to justify what you do rationally and also universalise the maxim that lies behind it.

But does that provide you with an absolute set of moral values, or a set that is relative to its cultural setting? The answer would seem to be that for each individual the moral demand is absolute, in that it is not dependent upon an assessment of facts or predicted consequences. But since no two people will have exactly the same 'good will', and will experience moral demands differently, it means that – in practice – there will be a wide variety of actual ethical practice. Viewed from the outside there will be variety; viewed from the perspective of the moral subject, all may be applying the same principles. In the end, morality depends on values, and it was Kant who recognised that values are something that we impose on experience.

Notice that the key for Kant is *autonomy*. If my intention is right, then I will not act at the whim of my senses, but with autonomy. The principles of my action come from my practical reason alone, they are not imposed on me from outside.

It is difficult to over-emphasise the importance of Kant for the whole development of ethics from his day through to the twenty-first century. *With Kant, the human reason and will stand supreme. Man takes his rational stand and no longer looks outside himself for external guarantors of moral rectitude. God becomes a postulate of pure practical reason, part of the structure within which the mind works.* It is a short step from this point to start to see the whole of moral value as something that is to be created by the human will and imposed on the external world, or even a philosophy in which human meaning and purpose plays the central role. As we look at Nietzsche, and later at existentialism, we are examining philosophical ideas that draw on the contribution of Kant. His was a Copernican revolution indeed; from then on, all values are seen as generated by man, not encountered by him.

Kant and democracy

Kant's moral theory depends on a kingdom of free, autonomous human beings, each an 'end', each responsible for legislating universally. This was a democratic ideal, from a period that saw both the French and American revolutions.

KEY ISSUES   Kant starts with the experience of moral obligation. What if people do not feel challenged in this way? What if they claim that they never feel they ought to do anything that they do not actually want to do? It is difficult to see how Kant's approach could ever persuade someone to act morally. If they already want to do the right thing, Kant's categorical imperative can be used as a guide; but if they do not, Kant would appear to have nothing to offer.

ARTHUR SCHOPENHAUER (1788–1860)   *-Profile-*

Kant had made the fundamental distinction between the world of objects known to the senses and the world of 'things in themselves'. Since all experience depended upon our faculties of perception, all that we could know was limited to that world of experience. But moral choice was not something given in experience, rather it was something known immediately by the pure practical reason: it was part of the 'noumenal' world. But for Kant, the unknowable *noumena* were the cause of the *phenomena* known to the senses, and it was assumed that there were actual separate noumenal entities out there in the world.

This was challenged by Schopenhauer, who argued that causality was limited to the world of phenomena, and also that the idea of separate objects was a feature of the time and space that our senses impose on experience. Therefore the world beyond the senses *cannot be divided up into separate things, but must be a single undifferentiated reality.* Today, we might call such an undifferentiated reality 'field' or 'energy', but Schopenhauer called it 'will'. It was the inside of the reality that appeared on the outside as the world of experience.

Now, this view makes a vital difference to ethics. If the reality beyond the senses is not differentiated, then fundamentally we are all part of one and the same reality. Other people are not separate from ourselves, except at the superficial level of sensation. There is a single 'will' operative in all.

This led Schopenhauer to argue that we have a natural compassion towards others, and we are naturally able to intuit the suffering of others and to respond accordingly. By doing this, Schopenhauer gave to compassion a basis in the structure of reality – *compassion is not unreasonable, nor is it simply one option chosen among many, rather it is a fundamental response to the most basic feature of reality.*

In hiw own life, Schopenhauer was far from compassionate, but that is another story!

Summary List

- Kant wanted reason to prevail over the ambiguities of inclination and experience. He therefore sought a moral principle that would be universally applicable, based on the pure practical reason that is exercised through our rational will.
- He saw morality as involved only with those situations where a person acts out of a sense of duty. To do something good simply because you enjoy doing it is not in itself moral. Morality is always a matter of conscious choice.
- He was therefore concerned with duty for its own sake, irrespective of the results of carrying it out.
- His categorical imperative states that an action is right only if the moral principle upon which it is based can be universalised without contradiction.
- For Kant, morality is outside the realm of nature. The good will is concerned with duty for duty's sake – and that cannot be supported by facts about the world, only by our own experience of a moral challenge.
- For Kant, autonomy is crucial. The principles of my action come from my practical reason alone; they are not imposed on me from outside.

Advantages of his approach:

- It conforms to what most people think of as morality.
- It is rational and certain, and does not depend on results or happiness.

Disadvantages of his approach:

- Most people do want to take the result of their actions into account, and may feel guilty if harm comes as a result of their good intentions.
- There is a certain arrogance about the view that one should stick to one's universal moral principles no matter what the circumstances. There may be occasions when it would be right to tell a lie, simply because by lying (e.g. to a terrorist about to carry out a bombing) one might achieve a greater good than by conforming to a principle of truth-telling. In fact, Kant is not as rigid as a straightforward account of his theory suggests, for he accepts that there are situations when circumstances make a general rule inappropriate – one of which is exactly that of telling the truth to someone who intends to do harm.

Questions

1. Explain the difference between a hypothetical and categorical imperative. Do you think that the categorical imperative, as presented by Kant, provides a sufficient guide to what is right or wrong?

Here it is important to include the first two formulations of the categorical imperative: that one must be able to will that the maxim of one's action shall become a universal law, and also that people should be treated as ends and never as means. Together, they do provide a very general, rational framework for assessing moral issues – but is such a rational framework enough to help solve the issues in practical ethics? That is a crucial issue here, and practical examples will help to bring it out.

2. An action is considered to be morally right, according to Kant, only if one can will that everyone else should be required to act on the same principle. Present examples to show whether you agree or disagree with his view.

This is essentially a more narrowly focused version of the first question. It is important to distinguish between the principle and the action itself when considering the implications of making it universal.

3. If you do not experience moral obligation, does that imply that nothing you do is right or wrong? Discuss with reference to Kant's ethics.

One may ask whether Kant, in basing ethics on the 'good will', made morality dependent upon an individual person's moral and rational sensitivity. One might also bring in the three postulates of the practical reason (God, freedom and immortality), which are equally implied by the moral sense, and vulnerable to its absence.

4. Kant's ethical theory is based on the autonomy of the moral choice, rather than on the predicted results of an action. Taking as an example one moral issue you have studied, say whether you think Kant's is a suitable starting point for an ethical discussion of that issue, giving your reasons.

Debate Topics

● Is it realistic to treat everyone as an end, rather than a means?
● 'Good will' is not universal. Discuss.

11 Morality and Power

Friedrich Nietzsche (1844–1900) is probably one of the most fascinating and challenging philosophers of modern times. He had the courage to attack key features of the philosophy and religion of his day, and to raise absolutely fundamental questions. His writing is not easy: he distrusted systems of thought, and preferred to hone his insights into short, vivid images. Often his purpose is clearest in his strings of aphorisms (short, pithy statements). Here we shall concentrate on the key features of his ethical thinking, but relating these where necessary to his overall views.

1 Background

In order to appreciate the force of Nietzsche's arguments, one needs to be aware of his background. He was brought up in a religious household (his father was a Lutheran pastor) and he was therefore very familiar with Christian ideas of morality and sin, and was taught that humankind was fundamentally 'fallen'. In other words, in order to receive grace and salvation, a person must first confess that he or she is a sinner, unworthy of God's love. Without God's grace, human beings can achieve nothing. Nietzsche's view of Christian morality is therefore coloured by this very negative assessment of humankind in its natural state.

In terms of philosophy, one can see Nietzsche within a tradition of continental thought that continued Kant's emphasis on the role of the subject self in interpreting and giving structure to the world of experience, and in freely willing and choosing – a tradition that included, for example, Schopenhauer and Fichte.

It is also important to see Nietzsche in the context of the great systems of thought of the nineteenth century – particularly those of Hegel and Marx. Although his approach is very different from theirs, he too thought in terms of an onward process of change. He was also aware of evolution and development and the newly enhanced view of humankind within the natural order. He did not see humankind as fixed, but in a process of becoming. There is a sense running through much nineteenth-century thought that humankind has a destiny waiting to be shaped.

2 God is dead

> **KEY ISSUE** In the opening section of Nietzsche's book *Thus Spoke Zarathustra* (1883–5) the prophet Zarathustra comes down from his mountain retreat and is amazed to find that people are not aware that God is dead.

Nietzsche saw the earth as floating free from the constraints of the old theistic structures. The sense of purpose for which Aquinas had argued was something that Nietzsche saw as having vanished from the intellectual world of his day. His task, then, is to examine a world without God, and a world within which humankind is at the leading edge of evolution. To do that, he requires two things: courage to face reality, and a desire to establish a new sense of direction now that there is no God to provide it. Two of his aphorisms at the opening of *Twilight of the Idols* (1888) express this:

> Even the bravest of us rarely has the courage for what he really *knows* …
> Formula of my happiness: a Yes, a No, a straight line, a *goal* …

The direction he finds, in the absence of God, is the next stage in the evolution of humankind, what he terms the 'overman', or (as it is generally translated) 'Superman':

> Man is a rope, fastened between animal and Superman – a rope over an abyss.
>
> Thus Spoke Zarathustra, *Section 4*

If the direction in which humankind is moving is from animal to Superman, then this will have profound implications for ethics. Rather than requiring morality to conform to a God-given fixed structure, or to an assessment of anticipated benefits, moral assessment is to be made in terms of the direction in which humankind is headed.

3 Willing the Superman

> I teach you the Superman. Man is something that should be overcome. What have you done to overcome him?
>
> All creatures hitherto have created something beyond themselves: and do you want to be the ebb of this great tide, and return to the animals rather than overcome man?
>
> The Superman is the meaning of the earth. Let your will say: the Superman *shall be* the meaning of the earth.
>
> Thus Spoke Zarathustra, *Section 3*

This last statement is crucial for Nietzsche's ethics. Following Kant and Schopenhauer, Nietzsche sees the will as the point at which morality comes into play. He is asking people to choose – to will – that Superman be the meaning of the earth. It is not a matter of *proving* it to be so, but *willing* it to be so. Once that step is taken, it is important that people should will the future of the earth, and not try to locate their personal goals in some heavenly realm. Nietzsche called those who were concerned mainly with spiritual things and with rewards after death as the 'afterworldsmen', and he regarded them as a threat to his new positive morality.

> My Ego taught me a new pride, I teach it to men: No longer to bury the head in the sand of heavenly things, but to carry it freely, an earthly head which creates meaning for the earth.
>
> I teach mankind a new will: to desire this path that men have followed blindly, and to call it good and no more to creep aside from it, like the sick and dying.
>
> It is time for man to plant the seed of his highest hope.
>
> Thus Spoke Zarathustra, *Section 5*

The essential thing to appreciate is that Nietzsche wants to set aside all traditional morality and start again. He wants to go beyond the traditional way of assessing behaviour, and to get *Beyond Good and Evil*, the title of a work he published in 1886. The phrase used by Nietzsche for this process was *'the revaluation of all values'*.

4 Master morality and slave morality

Nietzsche considered that the sort of moral qualities that had been promoted by Christianity – meekness, gentleness, compassion – were features of the morality of slaves, those who were concerned to help one another in a situation of helplessness and suffering. He contrasted such 'slave morality' with 'master morality', which he saw prefigured in the Greek ideal of the good life, and which included the sense of nobility and self-development. Master morality sought to develop qualities that would advance humankind; slave morality sought to develop qualities that would protect the weakest in society.

But he did not limit his moral criticism to Christianity. Nietzsche considered that the concepts of justice, equality and compassion, as they had emerged from the Enlightenment, and as they had been presented unchallenged as moral ideals and goals by secular philosophers, were equally the product of slave morality.

He considered that these two forms of morality gave rise to two different personal attitudes towards the world. Those who followed master morality would seek to develop themselves, to explore every potential to its limit, and even to give their own lives for the sake of something higher. By contrast, those following slave morality would be mainly concerned with self-preservation and protecting the weak.

5 The threat of the Christian ascetic

Nietzsche saw traditional Christian morality as a threat. It appeared to him to inhibit the natural development of strength and, by emphasising the weakness of man, it undermined a fundamentally positive approach to life which would be necessary for strength and nobility to be recognised and approved. Two quotations from his *The Genealogy of Morals* (1887) bring this out:

> To demand of strength that it should *not* express itself as strength, that it should *not* be a will to overcome, overthrow, dominate, a thirst for enemies and resistance and triumph, makes as little sense as to demand of weakness that it should express itself as strength.
>
> *1st essay, Section 13*

> The *sickly* constitute the greatest danger to man: *not* the evil, *not* the 'predators'. Those who are from the outset victims, downtrodden, broken – they are the ones, the *weakest* are the ones who most undermine life among men, who most dangerously poison and question our trust in life, in man.
>
> *3rd essay, Section 14*

The problem is that those who suffer think that they are to blame for their suffering. The concept of being a sinner haunts Nietzsche, for it creates a sense of guilt as a response to suffering, and this is encouraged by what he calls the ascetic ideal. 'Someone must be to blame for the fact that I do not feel well' is how he describes the thinking of those who are sickly, and they blame themselves as sinners for their plight. But the fact that someone feels guilty does not prove that he or she should be guilty. Guilt is interpretation, not fact, but it is an interpretation that Nietzsche ascribes to Christian morality.

Ascetic ideals are hostile to life. Nietzsche sees them within the Judaeo-Christian tradition and the secular forms of them accepted in the Western philosophy he saw around him. It is these anti-life ideals that he considers to be poisoning the life of the state.

Although he saw its influence as harmful, Nietzsche also recognised the power of the ascetic ideal – the slave morality – and asks why it should have gained such power. His answer is that it provides something to fill the void of a world without meaning, and gives some consolation in the face of meaningless suffering:

> For the meaning of the ascetic ideal is none other than *this*: that something was missing, that man was surrounded by a gaping *void* – he

did not know how to justify, explain, affirm himself, he *suffered* from the problem of his meaning.

> The meaninglessness of suffering, and not suffering as such, has been the curse that has hung over mankind up to now – *and the ascetic ideal offered mankind a meaning*!

And he ends with:

> ... man would rather will *nothingness* than *not* will at all ...

On the Genealogy of Morals, *2nd essay, Section 28*

In other words – and we shall return to this in the next chapter, on existentialism – humankind revolts from the idea of complete meaninglessness. It would rather accept a negative attitude to life than have no attitude at all. It craves meaning, even if the meaning it is offered is laden with a sense of personal guilt and unworthiness.

Note:

Notice the parallels between Nietzsche's criticism of slave morality and the ascetic ideal and Marx's criticism of the place of religion in society.

Marx – in a famous passage in his *Introduction to the Critique of the Hegelian Philosophy of Right* – described religion as:

> ... the sigh of the oppressed creature, the feelings of a heartless world, just as it is the spirit of unspiritual conditions. It is the opium of the people. The abolition of religion as the illusory happiness of the people is required for their real happiness.

In other words, Marx saw religion as holding people back from improving their actual conditions by promising them a substitute happiness. He judged that, deprived of such substitutes, people would face the reality of their situation and therefore be motivated to develop themselves and gain actual happiness.

Nietzsche is really saying much the same thing, except that his context is the nature of mankind and its movement towards the Superman, whereas Marx is concerned with the pattern of social and political change in terms of the class structure.

Nietzsche's criticism of Church morality is made clear in a section entitled 'Morality as Anti-nature' in *Twilight of the Idols*:

> The Church combats the passions with excision in every sense of the word: its practice, its 'cure' is *castration*. It never asks 'How can one spiritualise, beautify, deify a desire?' – it has at all times laid the emphasis of its discipline on extirpation (of sensuality, of pride, of lust for power, of avarice, of revengefulness). But to attack the passions at their roots means to attack life at its roots: the practice of the Church is *hostile to life* ...

The key question here is not whether the Church, now or then, actually took that view of the passions, but rather: What sort of morality allows natural human passions to be channelled creatively?

Nietzsche's answer to that is that we should seek a morality that encourages us to be forever going beyond ourselves. But recognise how radically different that sort of morality is from, for example, utilitarianism. To find a morality of this sort, we need to go back to Aristotle's ideas, in which the concept of good included ideas of perfection and nobility.

6 The eternal recurrence

> **KEY ISSUE**   The eternal recurrence is one of the more difficult of Nietzsche's concepts. What he is saying is that the Superman should be quite prepared to say 'Yes' to living this same life over and over again, just as it is, forever.

Everything in the world is linked together – happiness and sorrow, success and tragic failure – and one cannot accept some parts of it without accepting them all. For Nietzsche, the triumph of the Superman – and indeed, it would seem, of anyone who can say 'Yes' wholeheartedly to anything – is this absolute and positive affirmation of the world just as it is, however much pain it might involve. And in affirming this, Nietzsche returns to the idea that the Superman shall become the meaning of the earth. Whatever meaning and purpose there is in life, it is given that meaning by humankind. There is no God, no external guarantor or provider of meaning.

The eternal recurrence presents those who think morally with a fundamental question: Are you attempting, through your ideals and sense of what is 'good', to escape from the reality of the world as it is? Or are you prepared to say 'Yes' to the mixture of experiences, both happy and painful, that are the reality of life, and within that context exercise your will in order to shape your own destiny?

7 A challenge and a problem

> **KEY ISSUE** Nietzsche's ethical theory presents a clear challenge both to religious ideas of morality, and also to utilitarianism, Natural Law and any other attempt to give a fixed and objective basis to ethics.

The positive morality of the Superman is a morality that accepts life just as it is, and says 'Yes' to it, that develops itself to the limit, and is not deflected by self-pity or any substitute, other-worldly goals. The only criterion for moral action is self-transcendence – to develop yourself. But here there is a fundamental problem: What exactly should you develop?

We saw in Chapter 10 that Kant presented the categorical imperative as a principle that one should only do something if one can will at the same time that everyone else should be free to follow the same principle. In other words, one's action becomes morally good if done with conviction, and if it is without the prospect of self-contradiction if universalised. But that only gives the framework within which morality operates, it does not say exactly *what* should be done. The same problem occurs with Nietzsche. It is easy to see the sort of slave morality that he regards as weakening humanity. He is not happy with compassion, equality and justice. But what exactly is he expecting to put in their place for the majority of people? How is it possible for everyone to seek self-transcendence? What could it mean in practice?

> **Postscript to Nietzsche:**
> With the rise of Fascism in Germany and Italy, some 30 years after his death, some of Nietzsche's ideas were used to justify nationalist and racist views about the superiority of the Aryan race, views that led to the horrors of the Holocaust. Both Mussolini and Hitler read Nietzsche.
>
> In order that Nietzsche's thought is not simply identified with these later ideologies, it is important to recognise that Nietzsche himself – as far as we know from his writings – was not racist. The idea of identifying the development of the Superman with one particular racial group is foreign to Nietzsche's thinking, in which everyone and every group is required constantly to be going beyond itself. On the other hand, the later misuse of Nietzsche's writings highlights the problem raised above. His ethical thought gives direction but not specific content – except in the negative sense of having criticised justice, equality and compassion as being the product of slave morality. That, along with the very style of his writing, makes him open to a variety of dangerous interpretations.

Summary List

- In a world without God, one needs the courage to face one's situation, set one's own goals and say 'Yes' to life.
- Humankind is to strive to go beyond itself – to become 'Supermen' – and to allow that quest to give meaning to life.
- Christianity and democracy have promoted slave morality to defend the weak; Nietzsche wants a master morality to encourage the development of the strong.

Questions

1. Outline the distinction Nietzsche made between slave and master morality. Why did he see Christian moral teaching as slave morality? Are his criticisms of Christianity justified?

Use this as a basis for examining Nietzsche's criticism of both Christian and secular humanist morality. In particular here you need to give examples of those qualities that exhibit slave morality, and say whether or not Nietzsche's criticisms of them are valid.

2. 'The Superman shall be the meaning of the earth.' How does Nietzsche's view of the goal of human life in terms of the 'Superman' relate to his ethics?

The key issue here is the idea of going beyond oneself, and affirming one's life in doing so. It is related also to the conviction that meaning is not to be found in the world, but given to the world through the human will.

3. Life is always a mixture of pleasure and pain, success and failure. Would you be prepared to answer 'Yes' to living life exactly as it is, forever?

This gives an opportunity to explore Nietzsche's 'eternal recurrence' and his affirmation of life, as opposed to what he saw as the negative views of the 'afterworldsmen' who looked for some better world in heaven. Again, it focuses on the role of the will in affirming the self and determining the future.

12 An Existential Approach

KEYWORDS

existentialism – philosophy concerned with the nature and meaning of human existence

dialectic – the process of thesis, antithesis and synthesis that Hegel saw as the basic structure of change

Geworfenheit – Heidegger's term for the 'thrown-ness': the fact that we are born into a particular set of circumstances

1 Introduction

If we review for a moment the bases upon which philosophers have sought to establish ethical theories, we find that they are:

- the sense of justice within society;
- the quest for happiness;
- the structure and purpose of the natural order;
- the emotions, and our natural sense of altruism;
- agreements between people;
- the expected results of action;
- the pure practical reason;
- the will.

The first, third, fifth and sixth of these are independent of an individual's moral sensitivities; they attempt to give an overall way of assessing moral goodness which, through rational argument, people might agree together. The second is based on Aristotle's view of what constituted the good life, and the sense of the potential, both personal and social, that a person should strive to realise. The fourth of the approaches takes as its starting point people's natural sense of right and wrong, and their altruism – in particular the feeling that people in need ought to be helped, even at the cost of one's own immediate happiness. Such emotions suggest what ought to be done.

But in all of these there is the problem of trying to establish an 'ought' from an 'is'. We saw how both Hume and G E Moore used this as a major criticism of existing moral systems. The good cannot be defined in terms of structure, emotion, agreement or results, because it would then be possible to go on and ask if and why that structure, emotion, agreement or result was itself 'good', and so on *ad infinitum*. In other words, there needs to be some intuition of 'good', simple and indefinable, to underpin all such systems.

The remaining possibilities we looked at for establishing a basis of ethics were therefore the pure practical reason (Kant) or the will (Schopenhauer or – as we saw in the last chapter – Nietzsche). Following this line of thinking, we take responsibility for our actions and for shaping our future. We do not try to discover what is right and good and then apply it to ourselves, allowing it to determine what we want to do. Rather, it is our reason or our will that determines what is good. Of course, there will be guidelines about the application of that will. So, for Kant, it is the categorical imperative; for Nietzsche, it is the responsibility to go beyond oneself.

But in all these theories there is a balance between the individual and the society within which he or she lives. Some emphasise the role of society – ethics being established by mutual agreement, or by the assessment of those results that offer the greatest benefit to the maximum number of people. Others (e.g. Kant and Nietzsche) start with the individual, and then show how that individual morality relates to society – in Kant's case by thinking of everyone as 'ends' rather than 'means'; in Nietzsche's case, by seeing 'going beyond' yourself as part of an overall forward movement of humankind. *But should we start our ethical thinking with the individual or with society, and what is the right balance between them?*

It is this line of questioning that brings us on to **existentialism**, an approach to these questions that is generally regarded as starting a little before the time of Nietzsche, with the work of a Danish philosopher and theologian, Kierkegaard.

2 Søren Kierkegaard (1813–55)

> **KEY ISSUE** Kierkegaard emphasised the responsibility and challenge of individual choice in shaping people's lives.

The philosopher Hegel, who was very influential at the time of Kierkegaard, saw everything in terms of a broad collective process and movement. He is best known for his **dialectic**, in which a 'thesis' leads on to its opposite, an antithesis, resolving finally in a synthesis. Every aspect of human life was set within this overall process. In a sense, one might say that a person is part of a particular phase in social change, and is only to be understood by setting him or her within a social context.

Now Kierkegaard rejected this. He was a very religious man, and insisted that the key relationship was of an individual with God, and that God had given people freedom to make their own decisions. He therefore wanted to show that our existence is not something determined rationally, nor simply part of an ongoing process or abstract system, but was something quite specific. His philosophy starts with the individual and the values and choices that he or she makes.

He saw human existence as something that was created and shaped by personal choices:

> If you will understand me aright, I should like to say that in making a choice it is not so much a question of choosing the right as of the energy, the earnestness, the pathos with which one chooses. Thereby the personality announces its inner infinity, and thereby, in turn, the personality is consolidated. Therefore, even if a man were to choose the wrong, he will nevertheless discover, precisely by reason of the energy with which he chose, that he had chosen the wrong. For the choice being made with the whole inwardness of his personality, his nature is purified and he himself brought into immediate relation to the external Power whose omnipresence interpenetrates the whole of existence.
>
> Either/Or (1843)

Kierkegaard is therefore generally regarded as the founder of existentialism. This is a school of philosophy that is concerned with the nature of human existence and its meaning. It is particularly involved with the idea – central to Kierkegaard – that we have an active part to play in shaping ourselves, and that life is a constant process of becoming, in which our decisions are the agents of change.

Kierkegaard recognised, however, that taking such responsibility was not easy. He saw our freedom as something quite terrifying. It was an act of faith, a leap in the dark, to make a choice; and yet one could not escape from it. He regarded those (e.g. Hegel) who formed abstract schemes of thought in which to comprehend life and place every action in an overall pattern as in some way escapist. The real challenge of life was not in such speculation, nor in a structure that could guarantee that a decision was right, but in the actual process of acting and making choices. In other words, his challenge to ethical thinking is that one cannot understand moral choice by standing back and assessing it, but only by engaging in choices, conscious of the freedom to make a difference and to shape ourselves.

Kierkegaard regarded becoming an individual as a challenge, and believed that a person's 'good' was whatever enables him or her to become a true individual.

3 Martin Heidegger (1889–1976)

KEY ISSUE   Being yourself when faced with the particular circumstances of life and the roles that are imposed upon you by society.

Kierkegaard was a religious man, but one who felt that God had given to the individual the terrifying prospect of individual responsibility and choice. By contrast, Heidegger (like Nietzsche before him) approached the situation of human awareness and choice from an atheistic point of view. But there is another important difference: Kierkegaard presents the sort of ethical choices we make as though each of them is absolute and free; Heidegger recognised that most of our choices relate to existing relationships and commitments that are already established and presented to us. Thus, for Heidegger, we start from that given set of circumstances in which we find ourselves. These are not part of some divine plan, but are just given as an accident of birth. His term for this is 'thrown-ness' (**Geworfenheit**). From the moment of our birth we are given a set of conditions within which to live – we have not chosen them, they are just there. We are part of the world, and our choices are made as part of that world.

As we face other people, we form an image of them in our mind. That image is not the actual person (we cannot know them fully) but is like a mask we impose on them. One might think in terms of those who perform a function – being a milkman, a solicitor, an accountant, a shop assistant. The person I meet is far more than that social function, but nevertheless, that is all I know at present, and therefore I react to them on that basis. Equally, of course, a person may have the mask of 'wife', 'husband', 'son', 'daughter', 'lover', 'stranger' or 'enemy'. And, of course, as they look at us, other people project onto us the same sort of masks. When I come to make choices, when I act, how should I behave? Should I conform to what other people expect of me? Should I play at being what they expect? If so, do I lose my integrity? *What is the real me, beneath these masks and social roles? How can I live an authentic existence?*

These are the key questions for an existential approach to life and in particular to ethics. Existentialism combines a sense of the importance of exercising the will (as Nietzsche) and of recognising the freedom that choice implies (as Kierkegaard) but it also recognises that we do not exercise our wills, nor are we free, in a vacuum. We are thrown into life, into a particular set of circumstances. We are given a set of roles to perform, and we realise that our lives are seen in a limited way by others. In the light of all this, I need to escape the expectation of others and affirm my own authentic existence and freedom.

There is an additional motivation to start taking responsibility for our lives, and that is the fact of death. Heidegger makes the point that it is anxiety in the face of the inevitability of death, and therefore the very limited nature of our life, that motivates us. *In other words, there is a thrown-ness about our being born and about the prospect of our own death. The challenge is to know how to achieve our authentic existence in the brief space in between!*

4 Jean-Paul Sartre (1905–80)

KEY ISSUE   Existence comes before essence.

Like Heidegger, Sartre emphasised the creative role of an individual in shaping himself or herself. He did this by emphasising that existence – for human beings – comes before essence.

On the other hand, if you consider any inanimate object that is the product of human design, it is clear that the essence of that object (be it a car or a television, for example) was determined before it came into existence. After all, people do not simply create objects and then wonder what to do with them; a car is created as a car – that is its essence, and that determines what will be done with it once it comes into existence. For all such objects, their essence precedes their existence.

> **Note:**
> If we think about Aquinas' Natural Law approach to ethics, we see that he considered essence to precede existence. Thus any action has a purpose, and that purpose is an inherent part of its design or function. An action is morally right if it fulfils its allotted purpose. In this case, of course, Aquinas believed in a purposeful creator God, and therefore he assumed that everything is created with a purpose that it should fulfil. But Sartre takes an atheistic position. There is no generalised sense of purpose or design that can automatically be applied to objects, events or people.

Sartre took the view that human beings, in what they do and the choices they make, shape their own lives. There is no fixed 'essence' of me that I must discover and live up to. Rather, 'I' am something that will develop a particular character, an essence, as I go through life. My essence grows through my existence. In his famous phrase, which sums up what existentialism is about: *Existence precedes essence.*

But Sartre held that we choose our emotions and our motivations, and that these may be traced back to an 'original choice' that is the basis of motivation and which must therefore itself be unmotivated. But such a choice would be absurd. Therefore, however reasonable and directed subsequent choices and motives would seem to be, all our life is fundamentally based on the absurd. It cannot be rationally justified in terms of anything else.

Like Heidegger, it is important for Sartre that a person should not simply accept the roles that others might allocate, but should allow his or her sense of self to expand outwards to take in the things that are experienced.

Sartre sees human consciousness as '*être-pour-soi*' (being for itself), which is contrasted with the things of which we are conscious, which are '*être-en-soi*' (being in itself). This distinction is very important, for it characterises two different ways of being in the world. It is possible to become aware of the external world, to reflect upon it and relate to it in such a way that it becomes part of one's own consciousness: *être-pour-soi*. On the other hand, it is possible to refuse to take any active engagement with experience, and simply accept the roles that other people impose on you. In this case, you become an object: *être-en-soi*.

In the act of choosing, according to Sartre, you make clear the values that you hold for humankind in general:

> In fact, in creating the man that we want to be, there is not a single one of our acts which does not at the same time create an image of man as we think he ought to be. To choose to be this or that is to affirm at the same time the value of what we choose, because we can never choose evil. We always choose the good, and nothing can be good for us without being good for all.
>
> Existentialism and Human Emotions, *1957*

The existential task is to develop and take in new experiences, shaping oneself all the time. Life is a challenge and a project. In practice, however, Sartre took the view that one should allow to everyone else the freedom that one wished for oneself, thus creating a basis of mutual respect between oneself and other people. This approach provides the framework within which the self is to be developed.

5 Ethical implications of the existentialist approach

So far we have looked at the sort of views about human life and its choices that characterise existentialism. Clearly these have implications for ethics. First of all, it is clear that individuals have their own project, and therefore that the choices they make will reflect that. Existentialism therefore rejects the imposition of moral codes, rather, each person has to decide for himself or herself. It is most important to reject all attempts to have masks or images imposed on us; we should be free to reject all conventions.

For Sartre, the fact that God does not exist and that we are free to make our own choices does not provide mankind with an easy option:

> The existentialist ... thinks it very distressing that God does not exist, because all possibility of finding values in a heaven of ideas disappears

along with Him; there can no longer be an *a priori* Good, since there is no infinite and perfect consciousness to think it. Nowhere is it written that the Good exists, that we must be honest, that we must not lie; because the fact is we are on a plane where there are only men. Dostoievsky said, 'If God didn't exist, everything would be possible'. That is the very starting point of existentialism. Indeed, everything is permissible if God does not exist, and as a result man is forlorn, because neither within him nor without does he find anything to cling to. He can't start making excuses for himself.

Existentialism and Human Emotions, 1957

It is clear that a person has to accept responsibility for his or her decisions, and the implication of such freedom is that it should allow the same freedom to others. Thus it would be inconsistent to reject conventions that other people might want to impose on me, but at the same time seek to impose them on others. On the other hand, this rejection of all external aids and structures, although it emphasises freedom, is not an easy option. It brings both responsibility and a sense of loneliness, for we have to find within ourselves the courage to make choices and live with the results. We are what we make of ourselves – and that can be quite daunting.

The context:
It might be worth reflecting on the fact that the period during which existentialism developed as a philosophy corresponded to the time when conventional ethical statements were being challenged from a linguistic point of view. The logical positivist attack on moral statements, leading to emotive and prescriptive interpretations of what moral statements were actually about, helped to move the climate of thought away from morality as existing 'out there' in some way, to seeing it as a human project, as an expression of human wishes, emotions or recommendations for action. In this, of course, meta-ethics matched up quite conveniently with existentialism. This fact, however, was not always recognised, since existentialism was very much a phenomenon of 'Continental' philosophy, while meta-ethics thrived mainly within the Anglo-American analytic tradition. What we may see, however, is that existentialism is the conclusion of a line of argument that goes back to Kant – that, over and against the world of my experience, there is an immediate awareness of my freedom to make choices. Those choices, and the freedom to make them, come from within myself as an experiencing and willing agent, they are not simply derived from the external world of experience.

I act within the world, I do not simply watch while the world offers me ready-planned options, or allow it to determine what I should do. If I think of myself as part of that external world (what Kant called the world of *phenomena*), then I make myself an object, part of other people's *être-en-soi*, to use Sartre's term. Once that happens, I lose my freedom; I become part of a determined system of cause and effect. My awareness of myself as a free and responsible agent disappears.

What existentialism keeps open is the awareness of the significance of what happens when a person makes a choice. It is a point of freedom and/or responsibility, an expression of that person's individual existence, and at the same time it is the point at which his or her values are expressed.

Summary List

- Kierkegaard emphasised the importance of the individual moral choice and its personal consequences.
- Heidegger pointed out that our choices are made in the context of the given facts of our life. We try to live an authentic personal existence in spite of the roles that other people might give us.
- Sartre went on to say that human beings shape their own lives and do not have a fixed essence. They become what they are through the choices they make.

Questions

1. The freedom of existentialism to create one's own values is an easy option. Discuss.

It would be particularly appropriate to illustrate this with reference to Kierkegaard, who certainly regarded existential choice as a serious matter, and a more profound one than simply whether or not to obey a rule or conform to social norms.

2. According to Heidegger, we are thrown into life with a particular set of circumstances within which to make our choices. We are also expected to conform to the expectations other people have of us. Does this imply that we are never completely free to be ourselves? How might this relate to the moral choices a person makes?

Although it is useful to start with Heidegger, this question leads on to a more general question about self-identity, and the way in which the choices we make reflect the sort of person we think we are. It can be related back to the issue of freedom and determinism, outlined in Chapter 3.

3. 'Existence precedes essence.' Discuss this with reference to the existential philosophy of Sartre, and demonstrate the implications it has for ethics.

Clearly, this question is an opportunity to discuss the existential view that we shape our character, and thus our essence, as we go through life, particularly through the choices we make.

Discussion Topics

● Would you want to marry an existentialist? What risks might you be taking? What benefits might you hope to gain?
● Is it ever possible to completely resist conforming to social roles?

13 Situation Ethics

KEYWORDS

casuistry – the application of general principles to specific examples

agapeism – (from the Greek *agape*) morality based on love

1 Introduction

In the 1960s, both in the USA and in Europe, there was a widespread reaction against what was seen as the narrowness of traditional morality. It was a time of social change and of a quest for freedom and self-expression.

One book which reflected that social change was Joseph Fletcher's *Situation Ethics* (1966). In it he opposed a deductive method of ethical reasoning: that is, he felt that it was unwise to start from fixed rules and then deduce from them what should be done in any particular situation. This method of argument is sometimes called **casuistry**, as we saw above in connection with Aquinas (see page 66).

On the other hand, Fletcher wanted to maintain what he saw as the fundamental feature of Christian morality, the law of love. He therefore argued that there should be a single and simple principle, in the light of which individuals could work out what was right for their particular circumstances, and the situations in which they found themselves. *He claimed that the only absolute rule was that of love. In any given situation, the right thing to do was that which love required.*

Of course, he recognised that people would not always be able to decide what was right without help, and he conceded that rules could help to inform a person's decision. Nevertheless, ultimately, it was not the rules that counted but the principle of love. Thus, where love demanded that a conventional moral rule should be set aside, it was right to do so. Rules could not be absolutely or universally valid.

To some extent, Fletcher can be seen as following a tradition within Christian moral thought. In the earliest days of the Church, the break with Judaism involved setting aside strict moral and social codes. The early Christians claimed that their fellowship was based on love, and that it was therefore able to transcend barriers that separated people of very different social and religious backgrounds. An expression of love taking priority is seen, for example, in the famous 13th chapter of 1 Corinthians. There is also the well-known saying of St Augustine that one should love and do what one wants – which did not imply freedom, so much as the trust that whatever was fully motivated by love would be morally right.

A similar approach was taken by others. The theologian Paul Tillich, for example, wrote a short book in 1963 entitled *Morality and Beyond* in which he argued that if there were no rules, people would always have to work out time and again what was the right thing for them to do, and that in practical terms this would be impossible. Therefore (like Fletcher) he accepted that there could be rules, but that they should offer guidance only.

For Tillich, religion was about a person's 'ultimate concern' – that which he or she held to be of ultimate value in life – and his moral argument here links moral choice to that ultimate concern. In the end, there is something higher than the morality of obeying rules, and whether it is one's ultimate concern or simply an absolute principle of love, it is the striving after some transcendent value that makes an action morally right.

In practice, Tillich's position is rather more conservative than Fletcher's, and is widely adopted (although seldom related directly to Tillich himself). It represents a balance between Fletcher and conventional rule-based systems, and is a recognition that rules are useful, but only when informed by and, where necessary, open to the possibility of being changed in the light of ultimate values.

2 The meaning of 'love'

The term 'love' is notoriously ambiguous in English, embracing everything from the Greek term *eros* (erotic love) to *philia* (friendship). Here, the sort of love spoken about is best summed up in the Greek term *agape* (selfless love), and a moral theory that applies love to each situation can therefore be called **agapeism**.

It is also important to recognise that love (in the sense in which it is used in moral arguments) is not simply a matter of the emotions. It is not the same as being 'in love', which may perhaps be regarded as a form of madness in which a particular object of desire utterly dominates a person's emotional life. Love, in the sense that it is used here, involves the rational as well as the emotional. It is the recognition of the value of the loved object in and for itself. It is – to take an expression from 1 Corinthians – not selfish. In other words, it is not a self-indulgent emotion that happens to have latched onto an external object, but a recognition of that object as separate from oneself but held to be of value.

3 Evaluating situation ethics

Reflecting on situation ethics, it would seem to have some very definite advantages and disadvantages, compared with what it saw as the more conventional moralities of the day.

Its advantages:

- It is easy to understand: you follow a single principle.
- It gives a person freedom to differ from the decisions of others without feeling that they have thereby done anything wrong, or that they need to give a full justification for that decision. In other words, it is flexible.
- It enables an emotional and rational response to determine what is right in any given situation. In other words, you don't have to follow a conventional moral rule, if that goes against your deepest sense of what love requires.
- It is based on love, which, rationally as well as emotionally, is a key feature of all moral systems.

Its disadvantages:

- The absolute law of love is still a law. Not everyone may be bothered, or have the strength of character, to start asking what love requires in a situation. All that has happened is that a multitude of rules have been replaced by a single one – and one that is as easily broken as any other. If someone is going to behave in a fundamentally selfish way, they will break the law of love as easily as any other moral principle.
- It is difficult to know how two people, who differ about what they see as the demands of love in a particular situation, can engage in meaningful discussion. There is no objective basis upon which one can say that this intuition about love is more relevant or valid than that one. In other words, there is a danger that it can lead to moral vagueness – with everyone (at the time when this view gained popularity) happy about peace, love, flared trousers, flowers and long hair, but nobody actually able to specify how such love should be made effective in difficult or ambiguous situations where a shared commitment to a moral position is required.
- It tends to fragment complex moral situations into the individual moral choices where love is applied. At some point, it may be necessary to stand back and take a cool look at all the repercussions that a particular choice may have. There may be times when moral reason demands that something is done which goes against one's immediate feelings, but which, in the wider scheme of things, might be seen as right.

Note:

Although we have examined situation ethics in terms of Joseph Fletcher and Paul Tillich's work, we should note that the debate about the place of rules as opposed to the particular situation has a long history.

Thus, for example, the positive aspect of casuistry, in applying general moral rules to particular situations, recognised that rules needed interpretations, and that no two situations were exactly the same. *The 'problem' with casuistry was not that it was attempted, but that it was imposed.* It was seen as the means by which external (and particularly Church) authority could be imposed on individuals – often with very serious consequences. (For example, in Thomas Hardy's novel, *Jude the Obscure,* Jude is prevented from working as a stonemason in a church when it is discovered that he is not married to the person with whom he is living. A moral objection to cohabitation is thus imposed on him, with no attempt to discover his personal circumstances.)

Equally, the rejection of Hegel's system by Kierkegaard was an attempt to reinstate the centrality of the individual and the creative nature of his or her choices. And Sartre's insistence, that in everything we do we create an image of what we think humankind should be, is another way of relating overall principles to individual choices.

Whereas Natural Law started with the general principles and then worked its way down to the moral implications of particular actions, so the existentialist insisted that it was from those individual choices that a scheme of values was built up.

There are two terms used in discussions of situation ethics that are worth reflecting on: relativism and proportionalism. Clearly, situation ethics will always be relativist, since it rejects the imposition of universal rules (other than that of love). Tillich argued for a proportionalist approach, which was that rules should not be set aside on a whim, but only when the circumstances were sufficient to warrant it. In other words, the balance between accepting general rules and following the unique demands of love in each situation was a matter of proportion, never itself an absolute rule.

Summary List

- Situation ethics argues for a single principle: the law of love – i.e. in any situation, do whatever is the most loving thing.
- Individual people and situations take precedence over general moral rules.
- There has always been a tension between the rule and the individual situation, and Fletcher's work simply reflects this in the context of Christianity and the social trends of his time.

Questions

1. Assess the strengths and weaknesses of situation ethics.

A suggested list of strengths and weaknesses is given on page 123. It is important, with a question like this, not merely to list them again, but to give an assessment, particularly in terms of which are crucial for deciding whether one should accept or reject the approach taken by situation ethics.

2. Do you consider situation ethics, as presented by Fletcher, to be a valid interpretation of traditional Christian ethics? Give your reasons.

Here one should consider how situation ethics compares with a traditional Christian rule-based approach in dealing with various moral issues, but also with earlier Christian views on the role of love, e.g. in the writings of St Paul and St Augustine.

3. If two people disagree on what is the most loving thing to do, are they both morally right, even if they do very different things in the same situation? Illustrate your answer with reference to at least two practical situations in which there is a moral choice to be made.

In giving an answer to this, it would be important to comment on the difference between general principles and specific rules, and to say which you consider to be the more important.

Discussion Topics

● Is it any more likely that people will follow a law of love than obey traditional moral rules?
● Can we justify absolute moral rules in a multi-ethnic, multi-cultural and multi-faith society?
● Can love ever be totally unselfish?

This last point could be discussed in the context of genetic conditioning: the 'selfish gene' issue.

14 Religion and Ethics

1 Introduction

Since ethics examines moral choices and those things that are held to be 'good' or to express the purpose or goal of human life, it is quite inevitable that ethics will deal with issues that are also the concern of religion. What is more, ethical theories are produced from within a culture and historical period, and are therefore influenced by the prevailing modes of thought, including those of religion. It is therefore likely that religion will influence ethics, even where the ethical theory is justified rationally, and so appears to be quite independent of any religious authority.

If we look back at some of the key thinkers whose work has been outlined in this book, we shall notice that many of them either wrote from within, or in direct opposition to religion or the moral principles offered by religion. Thus, for example, Aquinas was attempting to give a reasoned argument in support of Christian doctrine; Nietzsche and Kierkegaard were both reacting to a strict religious upbringing, although taking very different views of religion; and Fletcher's situation ethics was clearly a way of modifying a conventional set of religious moral rules to fit with other more radical religious principles.

Religions generally give teachings about the nature of the world and of humankind's place within it, and as a response to these things, provide sets of moral guidelines. As such, they are part of the material that the philosopher constructing a theory of ethics will want to take into consideration.

We need to recognise that the ideas of right and wrong, and statements about the nature of the good life, are based (consciously or unconsciously) on a general understanding of the world and of humankind's place in the overall scheme of things. Therefore it is impossible to ask 'Why should I be moral?' or 'What is the meaning of goodness?' without touching on issues that are also central to religious thought.

2 The relationship between morality and religion

How then are ethics and religion related? There are three possibilities:

- *Autonomy.* Morality (or ethics) is autonomous if it is independent of religion, in other words, if its principles are justified on the basis of reason or experience alone, without reference to religious concepts. That does not mean that such an ethical system is opposed to religion, nor does it mean that it cannot be held by someone who is also religious. It is simply to declare that the theory does not require any prior assent to religious ideas. Utilitarianism is autonomous. You can agree with its principles without reference to religion.

● *Heteronomy.* Morality is heteronomous if it depends upon religious beliefs, or if it has been devised in such a way that it presupposes ideas and values that are given by religion rather than being presented on the basis of reason or experience alone. So, for example, the Roman Catholic Church has a body of rules called Canon Law. (The word 'canon' comes from the Greek *kanon*, which means 'rule'). In the 1917 Revised Codex of the Roman Catholic Church, there were 2,414 of these canons. These attempt to deal with the details of behaviour, and to simplify the process of casuistry, by which the principles of Natural Law would be applied to individual situations. Rules of this sort are made from within a religious community, and are justified in terms of the authority of that community. From an ethical point of view, therefore, they are heteronomous – they are not the result of individuals' thinking about morality, but are either imposed on, or willingly accepted by individuals as part of their commitment to a religion.

● *Theonomy.* Morality is theonomous if both it and religion depend upon a common source for their principles and values. Western religions speak of the source of principles and values as 'God' (or *theos*, in Greek), so theonomous morality is judged by religious people to come from a fundamental understanding of God, without depending, for example, on the authority of the Church or other religious group. It could be argued that the idea of Natural Law is theonomous, since it is based on the idea of an uncaused cause as the creative source of all, and suggests that there is a sense of purpose in the universe and therefore a final end to which everything tends. As presented by Aristotle, such ideas pre-date Christianity, but as Aquinas uses them, they come to be an expression of his belief in God. The same source is used to provide the basis for both the ethical theory and the religious beliefs.

Each of these three has something positive to offer in terms of the evaluation of ethical theories from a religious standpoint.

a) Some arguments for moral autonomy

● Obedience to religious rules out of fear of punishment, or abdicating personal responsibility in favour of external religious rules, detracts from personal freedom and choice. Can you really say that you have made a moral choice, when you simply act out of fear of punishment? If you are motivated by fear, are you free?

● We live in a multi-faith culture. Different religions (or different branches within the same religion) offer different moral rules and regulations, and these may conflict with one another. If you are to make a personal decision, you need to use your reason to assess and choose between them. Such a choice implies a degree of moral autonomy.

● If God is omnipotent (all-powerful) and omniscient (all-knowing) then He knows what I am about to choose to do, and would be able to prevent me from making that choice if He so chose. If I believe this, then I cannot accept sole responsibility for my actions, since God is always an accomplice to my deeds, by making them possible. Moral responsibility requires freedom, and freedom to make decisions and act on them implies moral autonomy.

b) Some arguments for moral heteronomy

● Society is influenced by religious views. Even those who profess not to follow a religion cannot help but be influenced to some degree. Therefore one needs to admit that a measure of heteronomy is inevitable.

● As soon as you start to define terms like 'good', or use any language about value and purpose, you are dealing with ideas that have long been shaped by religion. You cannot (unless you are going to start from scratch and devise a new vocabulary) present a theory of ethics that is free from the influence of religion. It is more honest to admit this influence.

● It is one thing to come to a conclusion about what you consider to be right or wrong, quite another to have the courage and conviction to put such morality into effect. Only religion, it may be argued, can provide the inspiration to do so.

● Autonomous ethical theories depend on the general good will and reasonableness of people in order for them to take effect. It is one thing to argue that one should seek the greatest happiness for the greatest number, and to show how reasonable such a view is, but if a person is determined to act out of totally selfish motives, there is nothing one can do. Religion deals with the dark side of human nature, the negative emotions and rejection of reason. It may be argued that, without the insights of religion, reason cannot produce a workable morality, for it cannot deal effectively with human selfishness.

c) Some arguments for theonomy

● The human impetus for morality and religion has a common source in 'mystical' awareness, or at least in an awareness of things that cannot be described literally. Iris Murdoch, for example, has argued for a fundamental awareness of 'the good' as a basis for morality, and that such awareness continues even in the absence of religion.

● Philosophers from Schopenhauer (who saw a fundamental unity of all things beneath the multiplicity of sense experience) to G E Moore (who argued that the concept 'good' was known by intuition, and was simple – unable to be defined), have found their ethical systems resting on that which cannot be described rationally, but has to be approached through some form of intuition or immediate awareness. And this, of course, has parallels with religious experience.

● Without some form of fundamental religious or mystical experience, it is difficult to account for the sense of moral obligation experienced almost universally.

● A believer might argue that if God is rational, and if He is the creator of everything (including human reason), then autonomous reason, applied correctly to the world as we experience it, will eventually discover something of God's will and purpose. What appears superficially to be autonomous reason is therefore (from the believer's perspective) actually theonomous, for God may be thought to be found both within it and behind it.

3 Religious authority – the Divine Command theory of ethics

Secular and religious moral systems can often agree on fundamental values, for example 'love' or 'respect for people'. It is not the moral conclusions that distinguish the secular from the religious, but the methods by which they arrive at those conclusions and the ways in which they justify them.

The Divine Command theory argues that whatever God commands is good. It is linked to the belief that God is the origin of all goodness. Even if that is accepted, however, the problem is to judge exactly how one can know what God commands. If it is argued that personal experience is primary, the conviction that God had commanded something might be totally unverifiable to anyone other than the person who had the religious experience on which that sense of God's command was based. On the other hand, if it is argued that a command in the scriptures would count as authoritative, there is a dilemma concerning the way in which the scriptures should be interpreted (literally or otherwise) and also the extent to which scriptures are to be related to the particular circumstances, cultural and historical, within which they were written. In other words, even if something was commanded by God 2000 years ago, does that mean it is necessarily valid for all time and in all circumstances? Here the Divine Command theory is challenged by relativism, which would see religious beliefs and scriptures as coming from particular settings, and not necessarily suitable for universal application.

But there is another fundamental problem with the Divine Command theory, and that is the dilemma about which should be considered logically primary: God or 'good'. It is generally presented in the form that originates in Plato, known as the Euthyphro dilemma.

The Euthyphro dilemma:
This is so called because it is found in Plato's dialogue *Euthyphro*. In it, Socrates asks, 'Is conduct right because the gods command it, or do the gods command it because it is right?'

If you argue in favour of the first option, you simply accept that whatever God commands must be considered 'good': you have no independent way of deciding right or wrong. Problems occur when it is believed that God commands something that, in a secular context, you might want to argue is wrong. For example, there are cases in the Old Testament when God commands the genocide of enemies. Is the genocide of enemies therefore to be considered 'good'? You appear to be at the mercy of particular scriptures and their interpretation.

However, if you do not accept this and take the second of Socrates' options, there are equal problems. It implies that there is an independent standard of good, known to human reason, by which you can judge God's action and therefore declare it to be 'good'. But this is to create an authority over and above God, which is what the religious person will not accept.

It is possible to use this dilemma in arguing for a Natural Law approach to ethics. In other words, if God is the rational creator of everything, then the universe should display a rational structure and purpose. Human reason, in contemplating the universe, is thus (whether it recognises it or not) also contemplating God.

4 Ethics and the religious traditions

In order to appreciate the moral arguments presented from within a religious tradition, it is necessary to get some idea of the basis and authority upon which such arguments are founded – whether, for example, they are based on a Divine Command theory, or on the authority of a sacred text, or priesthood, or whether they are justified with reference to human reason.

Judaism
Fundamental to Jewish ethics is the *Torah*, with the addition of the Mishna (oral traditions, believed to have been given to Moses by God) and its commentary, the *Gemara*. Together these form the *Talmud*, an encyclopedia of rules and traditions, governing every aspect of life.

- The moral authority of this tradition is seen as divine in origin, but subject to interpretation and application to particular situations.
- It is clearly deontological, rather than utilitarian or teleological, since it is a systematic interpretation of duties towards God and towards other

people. In general, obedience takes precedence over anticipated results.
- Human reason is a vehicle for interpretation, but not – as in Kant – a primary source of morality. Interpretation builds up a body of tradition, and following tradition is important chiefly as an expression of loyalty and obedience.
- Reason itself is seen as embodied in the voice of God, 'calling' creation into existence. In this sense, there may be parallels with a Natural Law approach, since humankind is to align itself with the will of a rational, creator God. The *Torah* is seen as a fundamental element in creation, rather than being merely words.

Christianity

The ultimate authority for Christian morality is God's Will. But that will, it is believed, is known through the medium of Jesus' life and teachings, as recorded in the New Testament, passed on through the teachings of the Church and revealed through the inspiration of the Holy Spirit. *In other words, there are three vehicles by which the ultimate source of authority is known: scriptures, tradition and inspiration.*

Christians have not always agreed about how these three should be balanced. For example, during the Reformation, the reformers shifted away from using the authority of the Church, towards the authority of scriptures as interpreted by each individual. On the other hand, of course, scholars will readily point out that the scriptures are not divine edicts handed down verbatim, but are themselves part of the process of interpretation and tradition within the early Church. Hence, the debate may come down to the authority of a particular interpretation, rather than the authority of the scriptures themselves.

- Christian morality therefore depends on an interpretation of God's Will, rather than on unaided human reason.
- The process of balancing early interpretations of scripture with contemporary ones may depend upon a believer's idea of the authority given to the present-day Church by the inspiration of the Holy Spirit.
- Beyond all this there is the belief that what was revealed in Christ was actually the agent of creation (the *logos*), a rational principle behind the universe. This is a concept that had already been explored by the Stoics, and parallels the creative role of the *Torah* in Judaism. Hence there is the sense (as revealed in the Natural Law approach) that reason and revelation should complement rather than oppose one another.
- Historically, Christianity, in separating itself from Judaism, defined its moral stance in contrast to what it portrayed as the legalism of its parent religion. Hence the emphasis on the demands of love rather than obedience to tradition, as seen for example in situation ethics.
- Christianity has always regarded the conscience of the individual as a vehicle of moral insight. In this case, conscience is not an alternative source of moral authority, but depends on the belief that the conscience is given by God.

Islam

The authorities for Muslim ethics are the *Qur'an* and the *Hadith* of the Prophet Muhammad. As with Judaism and Christianity, Islam recognises that interpretation is necessary in order to apply these to present-day issues. An authoritative ruling is given by a meeting of recognised Muslim scholars (the *ulama*).

There is also the fundamental belief that Muslims should 'submit' to the Will of Allah, and that to do so is to live in a natural way, at one with Him as the creative source of all things. Such natural living is referred to as the *Shariah* (which may be translated as 'path'). Every child is considered to be born Muslim, even if, through the circumstances of their birth, culture or conviction, they subsequently choose to turn away from Islam.

● Scriptures, interpreted by the appropriate authority, are basic to Muslim ethics.
● There are parallels to the 'Natural Law' approach to ethics since Allah, as creator, wants everyone to 'submit' and live in a natural way.
● Muslim ethics is clearly deontological rather than consequentialist; duty in obeying the Will of Allah is paramount.
● Islam accepts a valid role for human reason, but does not regard it as in any way an independent source of authority for matters of religion and ethics.

Example

It is important, in giving such a brief summary of the basis of ethics, to recognise the danger of caricature. Thus, for example, it may be pointed out that Islam prescribes the amputation of a hand as the punishment for theft; a view that, baldly stated, may be criticised as harsh. However, the consensus of Muslim legal opinion on the matter limits this punishment in four ways:

● The thief must be found guilty at a public trial, after the consideration of evidence.
● The person convicted must be adult, must not be psychologically unstable at the time of committing the crime and must not have been coerced into committing the theft.
● Neither the thief, nor his or her family, must have been hungry at the time of the theft. If they were, then the whole Muslim community is considered guilty of neglecting its obligations towards the poor in this situation. (In other words, acting out of desperation is seen as mitigating circumstances.)
● Amputation is only prescribed for a persistent thief, and is not appropriate for any case where it is thought that there is a prospect of the thief being reformed.

(This information is given on page 100 of an article by Clinton Bennett in *Making Moral Decisions*, 1994)

These four limitations illustrate the sensitivity of the Muslim legal system to the individual circumstances of people who disobey the law, and highlight the role of the legal tradition within Islam.

Hinduism

Hindu ethics reflects a wide range of traditions and cultures, along with the beliefs and spiritual practices that sustain them. In considering ethical issues within the Hindu tradition, it is important to distinguish between those things that are grounded in fundamental religious beliefs and those that are the product of social traditions.

- The Vedic term *Dharma* refers to the 'duty' of individuals to follow the natural order of things, as well as the creative principle that gives rise to such order. Hindu ethics may therefore be seen as deontological, with Natural Law elements.
- One's *dharma* is socially defined, and also depends upon one's stage in life. Judgement about particular actions is therefore relativist rather than absolute.
- The recognition of social differences and expectations (influenced by belief in *karma*) is very different from the assumption made by utilitarianism that all people should be treated equally and have an equal share in the anticipated benefits of an action.
- Unlike the Western tendency to examine ethics primarily from the standpoint of individual choice, Hindu morality emphasises its social implications; a person's actions take on significance and value depending on his or her position in society and its corresponding duties.
- Ethical action is seen as a spiritual practice in itself (*karma marga*), leading the individual towards liberation.

Buddhism

There are fundamental differences between Buddhist ethics and those of the other religions we are considering in this chapter, which stem from the fact that Buddhism is not based on acceptance of, or commitment to, a fixed set of beliefs. Rather, it is a philosophy that invites each individual to explore the nature of reality, and to reach his or her own personal conviction.

- Although the teachings of Gautama and the scriptures within which they are preserved are treated with great respect, the fact that each Buddhist is required to examine and evaluate them implies that reason takes priority over scriptures and tradition. This applies to ethical principles as to all other propositions.
- Recognising that each individual is unique, some Buddhist traditions place emphasis on individual guidance from a teacher in matters of spiritual development, which include morality.
- Buddhists tend to speak of actions as *kushala* (skilful) or *akushala* (unskilful), depending on whether they stem from compassion,

generosity and wisdom, or from hatred, craving and delusion.

- As in Virtue Ethics, Buddhism sees action as arising due to personal character traits, which are themselves formed as a result of earlier actions.
- The doctrine of *karma*, which Buddhism took from the Hindu traditions within which it arose, does not totally determine actions or circumstances, but is one factor to be taken into account. In other words, everything arises in dependence upon conditions, and one's *karma* (the results of ethically significant actions in the past) forms one of those conditions.
- At a basic, or conventional level, lay Buddhists accept five precepts: not to destroy life; not to steal; not to indulge in harmful sexual activity, or to indulge the senses; not to speak falsely, or to deceive; and not to cloud the mind with intoxicants. These are accepted as 'rules for training', in other words they are hypothetical rather than categorical imperatives. In effect, they say 'If you wish to make progress along the Buddhist path of wisdom and compassion, then you should adopt these as principles to guide you'. There is no divine law-giver in Buddhism. Buddhist ethics is also shaped by the desire to cultivate four mental states: love, pity, joy and serenity.
- The process of training appears to be similar to that of modern virtue ethics. However, whereas virtue ethics looks to human flourishing as its ultimate criterion of what is good, Buddhist ethics has a goal that goes beyond any benefit to the individual self. Indeed, the idea of a goal of human flourishing would, for a Buddhist, be seen as a sign of self-centredness, and therefore be a sign of delusion.
- The goal, for Buddhists, is an awareness of the interconnected nature of all things, and to live in a way that reflects that awareness. It is therefore very different from a Natural Law approach, which seeks to understand the 'end' or goal of individual actions.
- Buddhist ethics is largely situationist, in that it recognises that individual circumstances, rather than general rules, determine the nature of skilful action.

Sikhism

The Sikh religion has always placed emphasis on equality. This not only contrasted with the Hindu caste system, but also sought to overcome the wider distinction between Muslims and Hindus. This is demonstrated in the Sikh requirement that all worshippers should be prepared to sit and eat together.

- The fundamental authority for Sikhs is the Will of God, as embodied in the teachings of the ten Gurus and the *Guru Granth Sahib*, their holy book. As with other religions, there is the need to decide on an authoritative interpretation, and this has led to the acceptance of the *Rehat Maryada*, a guide to the Sikh way of life, produced in 1945 by a group of Sikh scholars.

- The Sikh emphasis on equality has parallels with Kant's second form of the categorical imperative, in that every individual is to be treated as an 'end' in himself or herself. However, the basis of this equality is very different, since Kant's is derived solely from human reason.
- Sikh ethics are mainly deontological, since they are concerned with the duties of individuals. Even if a utilitarian argument might justify the Sikh position on ethical issues, for Sikhs the issue of right and wrong is given by God, through the inspiration of the Gurus, and is not a matter of assessing results.
- There are parallels between Sikh ethics and virtue ethics, since Sikhs believe that people are naturally prone to live in a state of illusion, dominated by five evil impulses: lust, anger, greed, attachment to worldly things and pride. They are therefore encouraged to cultivate their opposites: self-control, forgiveness, contentment, love of God and humility. Notice however that the ultimate justification of cultivating these virtues is very different. Whereas for modern virtue ethics the aim is human flourishing, requiring no religious underpinning, for Sikhs it is based entirely on the desire to follow the Will of God.

Note:

All that has been attempted to look at the general way in which religious and moral ideas influence one another, and to assess the degree to which ethical arguments can claim to be free of religious influence.

Since this book is concerned primarily with ethical theory, there is no scope here for explaining the ethical basis of each tradition in any detail. For that, students will need to refer to books on whichever religion they are studying, or to a general introduction to religious ethics such as *Making Moral Decisions* (1994), edited by Jean Holm and John Bowker.

The crucial thing to recognise, however, is the source of authority and the method or argument used by a religious person in coming to a moral decision. His or her conclusion about what is right might be identical to that of someone from another religion, or someone arguing from a purely secular or rational point of view. It is not the conclusions that distinguish religious and secular ethics, but the way in which those conclusions are reached.

Summary List

● Ethical theories raise issues about the meaning and purpose of human life, with which religion is also concerned.

● Ethical theories are developed within cultures that may be influenced by religion.

● Ethics may be autonomous, heteronomous or theonomous with respect to religion.

● Within each religious tradition there are sources of authority that provide the basis for its moral teachings. The balancing of these may lead religious people to come to different conclusions on particular ethical issues.

Questions

1. Martin Luther and others have taken a 'two kingdoms' approach to religious and secular ethics. This is how Luther presents it in his *Secular Authority: To What Extent It Ought to be Obeyed* (1525), as quoted in *A New Dictionary of Christian Ethics*, ed. J Macquarrie and J Childs, SCM Press, 1986:

> We must divide all the Children of Adam into two classes: the first belong to the kingdom of God, the second to the kingdom of the world. Those belonging to the kingdom of God are all true believers in Christ and are subject to Christ and to gospel of the kingdom ... All who are not Christians belong to the kingdom of the world and are under the law. Since few believe and still fewer live a Christian life, do not resist evil, and themselves do no evil, God has provided for non-Christians a different government outside the Christian estate and God's kingdom ... For this reason the two kingdoms must be sharply distinguished, and both permitted to remain; the one to produce piety, the other to bring about external peace and prevent evil deeds; neither is sufficient in the world without the other.

Discuss the value of this 'two kingdoms' approach to religion and ethics, saying whether you consider it an adequate explanation of the relationship between the two. Illustrate your argument with reference to at least one modern ethical issue in which you consider there is a significant difference between some Christian and secular approaches.

For those studying Christian ethics:

2. Which aspects of the teachings of Jesus need to be taken into account when interpreting his moral principles? Do these make it inappropriate to apply Jesus' moral teaching to those who are not members of the Christian religion?

3. Does the New Testament offer sufficient guidance for Christians engaged in moral dilemmas today? Discuss with reference to at least two contemporary issues.

4. Religious ethics is necessarily deontological. Discuss with reference to the perspectives of the religion you have studied.

This question needs to be based on a clear statement about the origins and authority of the ethics of the chosen religion. The student will need to show whether they were always based on an understanding of 'duty' and whether they were absolute. You could argue that virtue or situation ethics are a valid approach to religious ethics. There could also be a comparison of the deontological and utilitarian (or teleological) approaches, and the religious implications of each.

Discussion Topics

- Can ethics ever be completely separated from religion?
- Does religious morality call for higher standards than secular morality?

15 Conscience

The term 'conscience' may be used in both secular and religious moral arguments, and refers to an inner conviction about what is right or wrong. The main issues here concern the origin of conscience, its validity as a source of moral authority, and its place within a moral argument.

1 A Christian view

In the New Testament, the word for conscience is *syneidesis*. This refers to the pain suffered by one who goes against his or her moral principles, and positively to having a 'good conscience' before God. It is also described as the witness to the 'requirements of the law' being written on the hearts of those who are not under the law (see Romans 2:15) – in other words, conscience acts as a guide, even where specific moral principles are not taken into consideration.

It is also interesting to note from the same epistle (1:18ff) that the wrath of God is described as being revealed from heaven against those who go against His moral laws, and the justification for such wrath is that there is no excuse or plea of ignorance, since God's invisible qualities of eternal power and divine nature have been revealed in creation. The implication here is that everyone has a conscience that can respond, even if unconsciously, to the requirements of the divine law. In a sense, this presents conscience as part of a Natural Law theory, in that the recognition of basic religious and moral principles is built into the structure of the universe and human nature.

Thus, within Christian moral teaching, conscience is regarded as the voice of God within the soul. This is how it is expressed by the Protestant theologian Friedrich Schleiermacher, writing in 1830:

> We use the term 'conscience' to express the fact that all modes of activity issuing from our God-consciousness and subject to its prompting confront us as moral demands, not indeed theoretically, but asserting themselves in our self-consciousness in such a way that any deviation of our conduct from them is apprehended as a hindrance to life, and therefore as sin. ... conscience also is very markedly traced to divine causality, and, as the voice of God within, is held to be an original revelation of God; it is one of those inward experiences which we may assume to be universal in this sphere.
>
> The Christian Faith, *Ch. 83*

In other words, Schleiermacher links conscience directly to a person's awareness of God, so that going against one's conscience is seen as sin. The implication here is that conscience is the product of revelation rather than reason. Although reason may subsequently justify moral actions that have been prompted by conscience, that prompting itself comes from God.

2 The secular conscience

In a secular context, conscience depends on two things:

● freedom;
● knowledge of the good.

Without freedom, conscience makes no sense. It is not logical to have an inner conviction that you ought to do something that is impossible. But equally, conscience implies some innate knowledge of 'the good'. Without that, conscience could prompt no specific action.

a) The origin of conscience

From the religious standpoint, conscience is the voice of God. But what other explanations can be given for this innate sense of right and wrong?

One possibility is that all our moral views are *socially and culturally conditioned*. Thus, for example, Hegel spoke of the 'spirit' of each age, which determined moral as well as cultural and aesthetic awareness. If this is merely a conscious awareness, it means that we judge what we should do in terms of the values that are held by the society within which we live. If, for example, we are utilitarian, we will consider the greatest happiness for the greatest number, but the nature of that 'happiness' will come from the values of our society. If, on the other hand, social values have become embedded also in our unconscious mind, then we may experience them as the promptings of conscience. In other words, our conscience reflects what society has taught us.

Another possibility, closely related to the first, is that our conscience, and particularly our sense of guilt, can be explained in *psychological* terms. During our early upbringing, we take on certain values and ideas that – even if they are consciously rejected at a later stage in life – continue to influence our moral awareness through the promptings of our conscience. Freud made the distinction between the *ego, id* and *super-ego*. In the simplest of terms, the first of these is the rational self, the second represents the self at the level of its physical and emotional needs, and the third is the controlling self, imposing rules on what the ego, prompted by the needs of the id, can do. Conscience, in this scheme, would be an aspect of the operation of the super-ego. A Freudian approach would therefore see the conscience as a product of the rules that we were taught by our parents, or other adults, in childhood.

A combination of both social and psychological factors influenced the work of Jean Piaget (1896–1980), who examined the stages of child development. He thought that, before the age of ten, children generally took their moral awareness from parents and others around them. After that age, they were able to develop their own set of moral principles, and have an increasing awareness of the purpose and social function of morality. This approach saw the development of conscience as natural, but as influenced by external factors.

A further possibility is that we have an *innate sense of right and wrong*, which does not depend on our early experiences or later conditioning. This is suggested by the fact that conscience is almost a universal phenomenon. The exception is the *psychopath*; the person who has no moral sense or feeling. The psychopath may be extremely intelligent, socially manipulative or charming, but has no awareness of other people as people, or any sense that their wishes or needs should be taken into account. Now, psychopathology is a complex science, and we can offer no more than a caricature here, but the assumption remains that 'normal' people have some innate sense of right and wrong and of what is acceptable behaviour. This is shown by the fact that they have a conscience and can show remorse when they have done something wrong.

b) Conscience as a source of moral authority

In Chapter 8 we examined some of the sources of moral authority. We noted that Rousseau held that there were two primitive emotions, one of which was a natural repugnance at the sufferings of others. He believed that this moral sense was innate, and was only masked by social convention. Similarly, Francis Hutcheson believed that people had a natural sense of benevolence, and that this – rather than reason – was the source of morality.

Bishop Butler considered that there was a hierarchy of authority within the self, with conscience at the top, superior to the appetites and passions. In particular, he considered that the conscience was able to overcome an instinctive concern for the self, and enable people to consider the welfare of others. He thought that everyone had a conscience and that, in order to know what was right, it was only necessary to give attention to it – to listen to the 'guide within.' As a Christian, he believed that God had designed the human personality to be controlled by its conscience and that to follow one's conscience was therefore to act in accordance with nature.

For Butler, conscience gave an intuitive awareness of right and wrong; it did not involve any form of calculation. He held that conscience had its own authority. Therefore some things – e.g. lies or unprovoked violence – are wrong, quite apart from any calculation of the happiness or misery that may result from them.

He believed that God created humans in such a way that their good will came from obeying the conscience that God had provided for their guidance. We should follow it because it is the law of our own nature and indicates the naturalness or unnaturalness of actions – and virtue consists in following nature. This means that, in the long run, conscience is not going to run counter to a natural sense of self-love, since it will serve one's own good.

One criticism of Butler, made by Elizabeth Anscombe (in 'Modern Moral Philosophy', *Philosophy*, 1958), is that he does not take into account that, in the name of conscience, people may do the vilest things. Butler assumes that conscience, having been given by God in order to direct the self, will always be good. He does not consider that it may be distorted or evil. This raises a fundamental question: How do you decide between two conflicting consciences?

G E Moore, in claiming that 'good' could not be defined, nevertheless insisted that people knew what it meant – and that, of course, implies some innate sense or intuition. If conscience gives us an innate sense of right and wrong, this takes priority over logical arguments that justify moral choice. In this sense, conscience becomes the starting point of morality, for without a sense of right and wrong, moral issues and arguments would never arise.

Conscience is also related closely to the idea of *integrity*. If we do one thing whilst believing that we should really be doing another, conscience is the vehicle of that intuition. At the same time, what is being challenged is the fact that we are not acting with integrity. *Integrity implies a good conscience.* In so far as personal integrity is seen as a valid goal for human life, it adds to the significance and authority of conscience.

c) The conscience and moral arguments

A moral argument is the rational examination of issues of right and wrong. Take, for example, utilitarianism. On the principle of utility – seeking the greatest happiness for the greatest number – it assesses a situation and makes a calculation about how happiness might be maximised. But that does not in itself define what is good, it merely organises how what we already know to be good might best be brought about. This was why G E Moore insisted that it needed to be supplemented (as the utilitarian Sidgwick had done) by a basic intuition of 'good'. Without some such intuition, it fell into the trap of trying to argue for an 'ought' on the basis of an 'is'.

If we look at the Natural Law approach to ethics – where ideas of right and wrong are related to the end or purpose for which something has been created – we find that Aquinas (in *Summa Theologica*) claimed that there are in fact *two* ways to act badly: one is to do what is known to be wrong, and the other is to go against one's own conscience. For Aquinas the conscience was the natural ability, given to humankind by God, to understand and apply moral principles. It could be mistaken, however, if the person either misunderstood or was ignorant of a moral rule, or if he or she did not realise that the rule should apply to their particular situation. Although conscience is not infallible, therefore, Aquinas still considers it to be authoritative.

Even though it may be authoritative, notice that conscience is not independent of a basic understanding of the nature of reality – as created by God, for example, and as having a natural 'end' or purpose. Thus, conscience is more like a skill than a body of knowledge; it is the natural and intuitive skill of being able to understand and apply moral principles.

Clearly, for Christian theologians, the idea of conscience is closely linked to that of God as creator. John Henry Newman (1801–90) followed Aquinas in seeing conscience as the ability to appreciate and apply moral principles, but he was closer to Bishop Butler in seeing it as intuitive, rather than rational. Its function was to stimulate and inform the process of moral decision-making. The feelings associated with conscience – guilt or shame, for example – are those of men and women who recognise that they are responsible to God (as ruler and judge) for their actions.

But this leads to an additional question: Is it ever right for one's conscience to overrule one's rationally argued ethical position? In other words, it could be argued that conscience should inform the process of rational ethical thought, but it should not take priority. Butler and others would claim that conscience is superior, while those who see it as socially acquired may well consider it less important than reason for deciding ethical matters.

In general, therefore, we see that conscience, or the innate knowledge of right and wrong, is not only compatible with moral arguments, but is seen as lying behind them. It is because we have a conscience that it makes sense to engage in moral arguments.

Summary List

- Conscience – the innate sense of right and wrong – may be described, from a religious perspective, as the 'voice of God' within the soul.
- It is possible to argue that the almost universal experience of conscience is the product of social or psychological conditioning.
- Conscience, as a source of moral awareness, is recognised by a broad range of ethical thinkers, especially those who base their work on emotion or a natural 'moral sense'.
- In general, moral awareness through the activity of the conscience is seen as a source of values and moral intuitions operating prior to the formulation of rational arguments. Moral arguments often result from the reflection on such moral intuitions.

Questions

1. Whatever the situation in law, a person is generally considered to be morally guilty or innocent not just because of *what* he or she has done, but *why*. Discuss the role of motive and personal integrity in assessing moral praise or blame, with special reference to the role of conscience.
2. Is conscience a necessary part of an ethical view of life? Discuss.

In answering the questions above, it might be worth reflecting on those ethical theories – e.g. utilitarianism – that give a method of assessing what is right without direct reference to motive or conscience.

3. Assess the view that one must always follow one's conscience.

This question is very broad. But it gives scope for examining a number of ethical theories, asking of each of them if one ought to go against the principles it sets down at the prompting of one's conscience. It would be important to illustrate an answer with a number of situations where conscience might come into conflict with obedience to some general rule, or where conscience suggests that one ought to keep to a rule, even if the result of doing so is against what one might want. It also gives scope for examining the possible origins of conscience, as an indication of its athority.

Discussion Topic

● Is conscience the voice of God? How could you prove it to be so?

16 Virtue Ethics

Three ethical theories have dominated Western thinking over the last 200 years or so: Natural Law, the Kantian deontological approach and utilitarianism. The first and oldest of these, associated particularly with Catholic thinking and heavily coloured by Aquinas' use of Aristotle, roots its approach to ethics in the view that every act or thing has an 'essence' – that which makes it what it is and gives it a place and meaning within the universe – an essence given to it by a creator God. In secular debate, however, the arguments have mostly polarised into those based on pure reason, stemming from Kant, and utilitarian arguments based on the anticipated results of an action.

There is, however, another strand of ethical thinking that goes back to the work of Aristotle, and which is closely linked to the Natural Law approach: virtue ethics. Virtue ethics starts with the basic question: 'What does it mean to live a good life?' This is a key feature of Aristotle's ethics, and depends – as does the Natural Law tradition – on an understanding of the essence or fundamental nature of things.

Virtues are those qualities that enable human beings to express their true nature. Looked at in this way, it is clear that virtue ethics is really an extension of the Natural Law approach. However, it is an aspect of that approach that was largely neglected until its revival in the middle of the twentieth century. Today, virtue ethics stands as an ethical theory in its own right, and not merely as an extension to Natural Law. In a secular context, it examines those qualities that lead to human flourishing, and does so in a way that is quite distinct from other ethical theories, and which has been found to be particularly appropriate in considering women's issues and concerns.

1 What are the virtues?

What counts as a virtue depends very much upon the circumstances. Thus, for a military person, courage would be a key virtue. For a religious person, humility and obedience might be equally important. From a humanist standpoint, prudence and self-control might be key features of the 'good life'. Socially, one might consider the virtues of modesty, politeness or even being good-humoured.

Such qualities are called virtues because of the effect of exercising them. Thus they may not provide their own justification, but depend upon effects – so it is possible to argue that virtues are not themselves an 'end' to be cultivated, but are merely means to another end, namely the flourishing and welfare of society or of the individual.

Plato, Aristotle and the Stoics considered that there were four 'cardinal' virtues (from *cardo*, meaning a hinge) which formed the basis of the moral life. They are:

- temperance (or moderation)
- justice
- courage
- prudence (or wisdom).

The exercise of these was considered to lead to a life 'in full', expressing the essence of humankind. There are many other virtues, some related to religion (e.g. the Christian virtue of humility) and others to social function. But all share the quality of being character traits, or dispositions, to act in ways that allow people to live well.

A question:
After studying virtue ethics, ask yourself if it is possible to have virtue ethics without also subscribing to the basis of the Natural Law approach. Does the fact that both are based on a fundamental understanding of the nature of humankind, and therefore of what constitutes the 'good life' for humans, make them two aspects of a single argument?

There is a large measure of agreement between ethical theories on what sorts of action may be considered good. What distinguishes one theory from another is the way in which the argument is presented, and the criteria by which actions are judged. What is clear is that a Kantian may argue in favour of telling the truth, but will do so on the grounds that dishonesty will ultimately be self-defeating, and will destroy the very nature of the concept of truth. Equally, a utilitarian may argue for honesty, but only because it will, in the end, lead to the greatest happiness of the greatest number. The difference between these approaches and that of virtue ethics is that the virtue ethicist seeks to promote honesty in its own right and for its own sake, not as a means to an end, nor as a logical requirement of the universalising of maxims, but because human good requires the cultivation of the virtues, of which honesty is one.

Aristotle held that the only worthwhile thing in life was to cultivate the virtues – that is what 'being good' is all about. And this fits in with our usual way of speaking. If I describe someone as 'good', I do not necessarily refer to a particular action that I consider to be right, but rather that this person shows a quality, a disposition, a habit to behave in a way that I call 'good'. In other words, to describe people as 'good' is as much a description of the way they 'are' as a description of what they actually 'do'. That is the distinctive feature of virtue ethics: it examines those qualities which make for the good life.

2 Virtue ethics in Aristotle

In the *Nicomachean Ethics*, Aristotle is concerned to show that virtue is its own reward, and does not need to be justified in terms of some other benefit:

> ... lovers of beauty find pleasure in things that are pleasant by nature, and virtuous actions are of this kind, so that they are pleasant not only to this type of person but also in themselves. So their life does not need to have pleasure attached to it as a sort of accessory, but contains its own pleasure in itself. Indeed we may go further and assert that anyone who does not delight in fine actions is not even a good man; for nobody would say that a man is just unless he enjoys acting justly, nor liberal unless he enjoys liberal actions, and similarly in all the other cases. If this is so, virtuous actions must be pleasurable in themselves.

As we saw in Chapter 6, Aristotle saw 'happiness' (*eudaimonia*) as the goal in life, something that was sought for itself rather than as a means to some other end. And this happiness consisted as much in living the good life as in enjoying the good things of life. In other words, for Aristotle, happiness requires an active and thoughtful engagement with life, it is not simply given.

Hence he regarded the virtues as qualities that are to be cultivated, expressed through and reinforced by action. They are more like a habit to be acquired than a chance description of a single action. They also express the mean between extremes (see page 55). The classic example of this is his claim that *courage* is a virtue that represents the mean between *cowardice* (a deficiency) and *rashness* (an excess). It does not represent an average of people's behaviour, but a balance between two tendencies that could prove equally damaging.

Aristotle's views were taken up by the Stoics (see page 59). They thought that the quest for virtue, rather than happiness, would enable the individual to act in a way that brought him or her into line with the overall rational purpose that directed everything. The 'good life', for Stoics, was one that displayed the virtues that came from living in a way that reflected the *logos* of the universe.

3 The revival of virtue ethics

It is generally considered that a significant factor in the modern revival of virtue ethics was the publication of an article entitled 'Modern Moral Philosophy' by Elizabeth Anscombe in 1958. She argued that, since many did not believe in God, it was important to find a system of morality that could be based on the idea of human flourishing – what it means to live the 'good life' – rather than obedience to the rules of an external law-giver. She argued that Kant's idea that reason would provide a self-regulating system of morality (in other words, that we would recognise and respond to the demands of the categorical imperative) was not a sensible one, and that most traditional moral arguments – particularly Kantian ethics and utilitarianism – required some idea of an external law-giver to support them. She highlighted the fact that in most ethical theories the term 'ought' is the equivalent of 'is obliged to', and this implies that there is a law and thus a law-giver.

The result of her challenge to traditional ethical theories was a re-examination of Aristotle's idea of the virtues as a basis for a modern secular form of ethics. Going back to Aristotle, and thus to a pre-Christian ethics, we find that he used 'ought' in a rather different sense – as in (to use her own example) you 'ought' to oil a machine if it is to work properly. It is not that there is an external law to be applied, but simply that a machine needs oil if it is to function properly.

Virtue ethics therefore asks what is implied by saying that someone is 'good' or 'generous' or 'courageous'. It is asking about qualities and dispositions to act, rather than looking – in a legalistic fashion – at the possible rights or wrongs of particular actions.

One of the most influential books on modern virtue ethics, is Alasdair MacIntyre's *After Virtue*. In it, he defines a virtue thus:

> A virtue is an acquired human quality, the possession of and exercise of which tends to enable us to achieve those goods which are internal to practices and the lack of which effectively prevents us from achieving any such goods.

This is best understood by taking a simple example. Suppose I want to succeed as an artist. I might try to achieve fame by cheating, or assume that I can produce something brilliant without effort. But even if I fooled some people by doing that, I would not actually become a good artist. In order genuinely to achieve my goal, I would need to exercise the virtues of justice and honesty in producing and displaying my work. I would also need courage and determination to stretch and develop my skills. In other words, the virtues are what will enable me to achieve the good that is inherent in what I have chosen to do.

Notice also that MacIntyre says that a virtue is 'acquired'. It is not simply a matter of being born with certain qualities, but of working to develop and exercise them. If ethics is based on developing the virtues, it is open to everyone to try to do so, not limited to those who happen to find it easy or who are naturally inclined to develop them.

MacIntyre considers three different concepts of 'virtue', from three different periods:

- In Homer, virtue is what enables someone to discharge their social obligations. Courage, for example, is the key requirement of the warrior.
- In Aristotle, the virtues enable a person to move towards a natural or supernatural 'end' or goal in life.
- In the 18th century, Benjamin Franklin lists virtues as qualities that enable one to be successful.

Not only do each of these depend on some prior understanding of the goal of life, but each will determine what qualities are seen as virtues. Similarly, while humility may be seen as a key Christian quality, for Aristotle or Homer it would have been considered a vice.

Another approach to the virtues, taken by Philippa Foot (in *Virtue Ethics*, 1977) is to see them as correcting existing human tendencies. Thus, for example, there is a natural human tendency to self-interest, which needs to be corrected by the virtue of benevolence. She also made the distinction between the moral hero, who has to struggle to do what is right, and the moral saint, who naturally does what is right. She holds that the saint is superior, although the hero has the greater power of will. Notice how different this is from Kant's view. For Kant, to act out of natural inclination or disposition, rather than from a conviction of moral duty, is morally neutral. For him, it is only the heroic that counts – for the saint, being naturally good, moral principles are irrelevant.

4 Feminist ethics

Feminist ideas are associated particularly with social and political thinking, since they emphasise the way in which a male-orientated society has disadvantaged women, but they are also relevant to ethics. By looking at ethical issues from a woman's point of view, feminist ethics seeks to restore the balance in what it sees as a male-dominated way of examining moral issues, and thus work towards ethical perspectives that are equally applicable to men and women.

Virtue ethics was particularly attractive to feminist thinkers, since they felt that the traditional moral arguments, based on ideas of duty and right, were the product of a male way of looking at moral issues. They believed that they did not give adequate account of the qualities – such as care and compassion – that had important implications for ethical issues, and which were also seen as particularly relevant to the experience and concerns of women. In particular, much traditional ethics has been concerned with individual personal autonomy, which feminists see as a distinctively male trait, as opposed to a female emphasis on relationships and mutual support.

One key question for virtue ethics, especially in a feminist context, is whether we have a fixed 'essence' or are mainly the product of social or psychological conditioning. This was highlighted by Simone de Beauvoir who, in her influential book *The Second Sex* (1949), raised the issue of whether one is born a woman, or becomes a woman. In other words, whether those things that we associate with the feminine are natural or a social construction. If it is the latter, they may well have been imposed on women (and sometimes unconsciously accepted by them) by a male-dominated society.

Virtue ethics has particular value for feminist thought in that it invites a consideration of those qualities that lead to human flourishing (thus applicable equally to men and women), rather than concentrating on the traditional ethical arguments, which appeared to be underpinned by belief in a divine, male law-giver.

5 The distinctiveness of virtue ethics

Notice that, whereas other ethical theories tend to focus on the right or wrong of particular acts, virtue ethics is more concerned with the cultivation of qualities that express themselves in actions, but are not simply to be identified with them.

Iris Murdoch, in *The Sovereignty of Good* (2001), pointed out that we act at any given moment on the basis of habitual ways of understanding the world and responding to it, which we have built up over a long period of time. In doing what we do, we are unlikely to act completely out of character, but will have been trained by our life experience to respond to a situation in one way or another. Hence the crucial fact that virtue ethics considers the development of those qualities, the exercise of which will be good for human flourishing. They may suggest particular actions in particular situations, but cannot prescribe them.

Notice that some virtues – for example, courage, temperance and wisdom – are likely to be of immediate benefit to the person who possesses them, quite apart from the effect that they have on others. If being courageous is of benefit to me, it makes no sense to ask why I should bother to be courageous – as though it were something commanded from outside. If it is to my benefit, it is naturally something to be desired. The matter is less clear with a virtue that relates to others, such as charity,and therefore it makes more sense to ask 'Why should I bother to be charitable?' In such cases, those who consider virtue ethics are likely to look at issues such as the will (I do something because I choose to do it, irrespective of any immediate benefit to myself), or else they relate it to a general view of life (I accept certain things to be of value, and will therefore seek to achieve them). This last position reinforces that taken by Iris Murdoch, who related moral choice to overall views of reality, such that a particular choice was not made in a vacuum, but related to an understanding of life that had become habitual.

Most importantly, notice that the focus of virtue ethics is set on the nature of the individual who acts. Since virtues are not acquired instantaneously, but developed to the point at which they become habitual, it makes sense to say that a person can seek to develop moral sensitivity, by exercising the virtues in all the choices that he or she makes.

Summary List

● Virtue ethics explores those qualities that enable human beings to live well.
● A good person is one who displays and acts in line with the virtues.
● A virtue is a character trait or quality, indicating a disposition to act in a certain way – e.g. justly, honestly, kindly, prudently, etc.
● Virtue ethics is compatible with religious belief, but does not require the presence of an external divine law-giver.

Questions

1. Virtue ethics depends on a view of the essence and purpose of human life, and thus on Natural Law. Discuss.
2. Virtue ethics is the only alternative to a male-dominated morality. Discuss.

Discussion Topic

● Does virtue ethics provide a comprehensive moral theory, or does it need to be supplemented by one or more of the other theories? (For example, how might you decide between two courses of action, both of which demand courage or kindness?)

Postscript: Where Do We Go From Here?

This book has been concerned with ethical theory – with the general arguments and principles by which people have sought to establish a rational basis for the assessment of moral issues, and also with the consideration of those things that may be regarded as 'good' and 'right', both in terms of actions and the aims and purposes that motivate action.

Many of the thinkers we have considered here were actively concerned to comment on and shape the society of their day. Marx was not strictly accurate when he said that earlier philosophers had sought to understand the world, whereas he wanted to change it. There were others – Bentham, for example – who wrote out of their personal involvement in political and social issues. It is equally the case that ethical theory is of limited interest unless it can be seen to be of relevance to practical moral issues. The proof of ethical theory is therefore to be found in applied ethics.

In terms of the academic debate, applied ethics had rather fallen into abeyance during the middle years of the twentieth century, due to the impact of linguistic philosophy and its questions about the nature of language and the validity of moral statements. From the 1930s until the early 1960s, ethics was dominated by meta-ethical questions. In other words, philosophers were more concerned to ask if moral statements were possible, and how they might be shown to be true or false, than to ask if this or that action was inherently right or wrong. Indeed A J Ayer (in 'The Analysis of Moral Judgements' in *Philosophical Essays*, 1959) thought that people should not look to philosophers for guidance about matters of right and wrong.

Within a decade or so, all that was to change. Influenced perhaps by the radical political and social attitudes of the 1960s, the traumas of the Vietnam War vividly brought to life day by day on television screens, the Peace Movements, the development of alternative lifestyles and an awareness of the human threat to the environment, there was a demand for new approaches to ethics.

The traditional areas of ethics – sex and relationships, issues of life and death, the nature of law and political rights – were soon to be supplemented by others: feminist ethics, environmental ethics, business ethics. But there was also a growing concern among the professions for ethical guidance. This was seen particularly in the medical and nursing professions, where there was a clear need to define the moral expectations of professional conduct, and also to consider areas of medicine – for example, artificial methods of conception, or euthanasia – where medical and nursing practice needed to be guided by clearly defined principles about what would be acceptable to the profession as a whole.

By the beginning of the 21st century, the news was dominated by other ethical issues, particularly the moral justification of initiating war, the question of how to understand and counter acts of terrorism, the social and political issues raised by asylum-seekers and economic migrants, the effective use of resources in medicine and the protection of natural resources globally. There was also an overall increase in awareness of the relationship between religious and social attitudes and ethics – with an appreciation of the complexities of living in a multi-ethnic, multi-faith community.

What seems certain – as can be confirmed by looking at almost any daily newspaper – is that there will continue to be a flourishing interest in applied ethics of one form or another. The pace of social and technological change is so rapid that some professionals feel that they do not have either the opportunity or the expertise to take account of the moral implications of what they do. At the same time, largely influenced by the situation in the USA, the tendency is for those who feel that they have been hurt in any way through the negligence or malpractice of an individual, agency, or state, to have no hesitation in testing their claims in the court and seeking damages. Hence the wariness of professionals who feel themselves to be vulnerable to ethical implications in what they do, that have not been properly considered but which are potential openings for future litigation.

There is also a great deal of emotion in areas of morality, and this is not always harnessed to rational consideration. G E Moore may indeed have been right to say that some fundamental concepts, like 'good', are known intuitively, and it may indeed be the case that individuals and groups intuitively sense themselves to have been wronged in some way, or to have right on the side of the cause they fight, but, if that intuition is to lead to positive change (or, indeed, successful litigation), it needs to be backed by carefully reasoned and presented argument. Hence there is a very positive role for applied ethics in the future.

But whereas the practical implications of ethics may have a clear future, the same cannot necessarily be said for ethical theory. Much debate today is based on a combination of theories. Utilitarianism is still prominent in many ethical arguments, contract-based ethics is important in many professional and political situations, and on the personal front there is continued interest in virtue ethics, examining the human qualities that are cultivated by and expressed through morality. Very few are prepared to return to the days of Ayer and claim that moral language is meaningless – for when the meaningless becomes a vehicle for litigation it suddenly becomes both real and relevant!

And somewhere in the midst of all this there remains a fundamental quest for 'the good'. Writing in the late 1960s, Iris Murdoch looked at a world in which moral philosophy had become dominated by the effects of linguistic philosophy and also of existentialism. She noted that empiricism, as expounded by Wittgenstein and Bertrand Russell, had made ethics almost impossible, by arguing that moral judgements were not factual. Some assumed that psychology and sociology would supply all the details of personal motivation, rendering conventional moral arguments redundant. Murdoch noted that for Freudian analysis, objectivity and unselfishness in actions were seen as practically impossible, since the self is motivated by its deepest needs, especially sexual ones.

Others concentrated on the moment of freedom, of self-assertion and of living authentically. But where in all this, Murdoch asked, was there a sense of a complex web of values and virtues? It was almost as if, in surveying the moral landscape, there seemed no place for innocent moral goodness. Although she recognised that an existentialist approach at least offered a philosophy that could be 'lived in', she criticised it as tending towards egocentricity, with the human will taking precedence over the real world outside the self. She saw danger in its attempt to reduce all human virtues to those of freedom and sincerity.

Murdoch also highlighted the fundamental shift in ethics that came about as a result of Kant's 'Copernican revolution' (see page 92):

> The centre of this type of post-Kantian moral philosophy is the notion of the will as the creator of value. Values which were previously in some sense inscribed in the heavens and guaranteed by God collapse into the human will. There is no transcendent reality. The idea of the good remains indefinable and empty so that human choice may fill it.
>
> The Sovereignty of Good

Particularly when looking at ethics from a religious perspective, this great hinge in the history of ethics needs to be kept in mind. Looking at Schopenhauer, or Nietzsche, or Heidegger or Sartre, there is the human-centred need to create morality and value, to set a human stamp on the universe that would otherwise be morally neutral and impersonal. That is a view that, right or wrong, is fundamentally at odds with earlier thinking, both religious and secular.

Murdoch therefore returned to the most fundamental of questions: 'What is a good man like? How can we make ourselves morally better? *Can* we make ourselves morally better? These are the questions the philosopher should try to answer.'

In response to the limitations of existing ethical theory, she turned to the Platonic idea of regarding virtue as something that may be perceived and understood (rather than willed and created). She argued that attending to that perception – in Platonic terms, being aware of what is outside and beyond the shadows on the wall of our cave – can lead to the making of morally good choices when the occasion arises.

In this sense, she saw an 'objective' basis for morality, as for virtue. She linked this with great works of literature and art, in which the vision of the artist presents reality in a way that startles us out of the selfish preoccupations of our habitual way of looking. In all this, she sees the narrow concerns of purpose as inadequate to contain a sense of a good that is transcendent, much as Plato's Form of the Good was seen as transcendent. When she comes to define what she means by 'good' she says this:

> The Good has nothing to do with purpose, indeed it excludes the idea of purpose. 'All is vanity' is the beginning and end of ethics. The only genuine way to be good is to be good 'for nothing' in the midst of the scene where every 'natural' thing, including one's own mind, is subject to chance, that is, to necessity. That 'for nothing' is indeed the experienced correlate of the invisibility or non-representable blankness of the idea of Good itself.

> The Sovereignty of Good

In other words, she is saying that, if you try to explain 'good' in terms of something else – some ideal future, or universal happiness, for example – then you should be aware that ultimately all such things will turn to dust. Nothing in this world is permanent and ultimate.

But that does not stop us from having a sense that there are some things and actions that are simply 'good', even if we cannot define what we mean by that word, and while this sense of the 'good' remains, there will be a future for ethics.

Summary List

- During the last three decades of the twentieth century, there was a revival of interest in applied ethics.
- With increased emphasis on professionalism, and the need to justify professional judgement in the courts, ethics plays an important role in establishing what is to be regarded as acceptable practice within an increasing number of professions.
- There is an ever-growing list of issues, of daily and global concern, which require careful ethical thought if humankind is to flourish.
- The fundamental sense of the 'good', even if that cannot be defined, continues to inspire work on ethics.

Discussion Topic

- Having studied the various ethical theories in this book, reflect on and discuss which of them you find most credible as giving an overall account of what is right or wrong, and which you find most readily applicable to practical moral issues.

Glossary

a posteriori   used of an argument that depends on sense experience

a priori   used of a thought, or moral argument, that arises prior to, or is not based on, a consideration of evidence in the form of sense experience

absolutist   used of moral arguments that suggest that it is possible, in theory, to specify moral principles that can be applied universally

act utilitarianism   utilitarian theory applied to individual actions

agapeism   moral theory based on the application of love to each situation

altruism   the unselfish consideration of others

amoral   the term used for an action that, with respect to the person who performs it, is done without reference to any moral system

applied ethics   the term used for the application of ethical theory to specific issues

axiological questions   questions about a person's values

cardinal virtues   prudence (wisdom), justice, fortitude (courage) and temperance; Stoic principles of the moral life, found in Plato and Aristotle and used also by Aquinas

casuistry   the application of general principles to specific examples

categorical imperative   Kant's rational assessment of what is implied by an absolute moral demand (*cp.* hypothetical imperative)

compatibilism   the view that a measure of human freedom is compatible with an acceptance of the universal principle of cause and effect

consequentialist ethics   any ethical theory based on results, or the consequences of an action (e.g. utilitarianism)

deontological questions   questions about a person's rights and duties

descriptive ethics   the description of the actual moral choices and values held within a society

determinism   philosophical view to the effect that every act is totally conditioned and therefore that agents are not free

dialectic   the process of thesis, antithesis and synthesis that Hegel saw as the basic structure of change

doxa   Greek term for opinion

efficient cause   the agent that brings something about

emotivism   theory that moral statements are in fact expressions of emotion, either approving or disapproving of actions

episteme   Greek term for knowledge

eudaimonia   Greek term for happiness

existentialism   the general term for the philosophical consideration of an individual's personal sense of meaning and existence, and the overall view of life stemming from such consideration

final cause   the final aim or purpose of something

Form   a universal reality, in which individual things share

Geworfenheit   Heidegger's term for the 'thrown-ness': the fact that we are born into a particular set of circumstances

hypothetical imperative   a command to be obeyed only in order to fulfil some limited purpose, taking the form 'do … if you want to achieve …'.

immoral   behaviour that goes against an accepted set of norms

intuitionism a view that 'good' is a simple term and may not be further defined, but is known through intuition (associated with, but not used by, G E Moore)

logical positivism philosophical approach which described as meaningful only those statements that could be verified with reference to sense experience (and therefore concluded that ethical statements were meaningless)

logos Greek term for 'word', used of the Christian view of Christ as the 'Word' of God in creation, and used by the Stoics for the fundamental rationality in the universe

maxim the moral principle governing an action

the mean Aristotle's idea that doing right involves a balance between extremes

meta-ethics the study of the nature and function of ethical statements

metaphysical ethics an approach that sought to relate ethical claims to an overall view of the nature of reality (see e.g. Bradley)

moral behaviour that conforms to an accepted set of norms

Natural Law ethical theory based on the idea of a 'final cause' or purpose, which defines the proper use or goal of everything

naturalistic fallacy the error (as argued by Hume, G E Moore and others) of trying to derive an 'ought' from an 'is'

non-cognitive describes a statement that conveys no factual information; used of an approach to moral claims that relates them exclusively to the emotions and preferences of people who use them

normative ethics a consideration of the principles that influence moral choice and value, used of discussions of what is right, as opposed to descriptions of moral behaviour

preference utilitarianism utilitarian theory taking into account the maximum satisfaction of the preferences of the individuals concerned

prescriptivism the theory that moral statements recommend (or 'prescribe') a particular course of action

rationalist ethics used of any ethical theory based on reason

reductionism philosophical approach that seeks to 'reduce' everything to basic empirical events (e.g. thoughts are reduced to electric impulses in the brain)

relativist used of moral arguments that consider issues of right and wrong in the light of their particular social, historical or cultural context

rule utilitarianism utilitarian theory that takes into account the benefits gained by obeying general rules of conduct

teleological (approach to ethics) an approach based on the expected end or purpose (*telos*) of an action

telos Greek term for 'end' or 'purpose'

utilitarianism a consequentialist moral theory based on the 'principle of utility', namely the assessment of what will offer the greatest happiness to the greatest number

virtue ethics ethical theory based on human qualities to be cultivated and expressed through moral choices

Timeline of Philosophers

470–399 BCE	Socrates
c. 428–347 BCE	Plato
384–322 BCE	Aristotle
341–270 BCE	Epicurus
c. 334–262 BCE	Zeno
50–130 CE	Epcitetus
121–180 CE	Emperor Marcus Aurelius
1225–74	Thomas Aquinas
1588–1679	Thomas Hobbes
1632–1704	John Locke
1671–1713	Earl of Shaftesbury
1692–1752	Bishop Butler
1694–1746	Francis Hutcheson
1711–76	David Hume
1712–78	Jean-Jacques Rousseau
1724–1804	Immanuel Kant
1737–1809	Thomas Paine
1748–1832	Jeremy Bentham
1788–1860	Artur Schopenhauer
1806–73	J S Mill
1813–55	Søren Kierkegaard
1838–1900	Henry Sidgwick
1844–1900	Friedrich Nietzsche
1871–1947	H A Prichard
1873–1958	G E Moore
1877–1971	W D Ross
1889–1951	L Wittgenstein
1889–1976	Martin Heidegger
1905–80	Jean-Paul Sartre
1908–79	C L Stevenson
1910–89	A J Ayer
1917–81	John Mackie
1919–99	Iris Murdoch
1919–2002	R M Hare
1919–2002	John Rawls
b. 1929	Bernard Williams

Further Reading

By the same author:
Ethics (3rd edition) (Hodder Arnold Teach Yourself, 2003)
An Introduction to Philosophy and Ethics (*Access to Philosophy* series)
   (Hodder Arnold, 2003)

For applied ethics within the *Access to Philosophy* series:
Joe Walker, *Environmental Ethics* (Hodder Arnold, 2000)
Michael Wilcockson, *Issues of Life and Death* (Hodder Arnold,1999)
Michael Wilcockson, *Sex and Relationships* (Hodder Arnold,1999)

**For detailed, concise information about particular ethical thinkers
and arguments:**
Edward Craig (ed.), *The Concise Routledge Encyclopedia of Philosophy*
   (Routledge, 2000)
Ted Honderich (ed.), *The Oxford Companion to Philosophy* (OUP,
   1995)

**Many of the classical texts mentioned in this book are available in
paperback. There are also a number of anthologies, including:**
O A Johnson, *Ethics: Selections from Classical and Contemporary Writers*
   (7th edition) (Wadsworth, 2003)

Other useful books include:
Robert L Arrington, *Western Ethics: an historical introduction*
   (Blackwell, 1998)
A J Ayer, 'The Analysis of Moral Judgements' in *Philosophical Essays*
   (1959)
Ray Billington, *Living Philosophy: An Introduction to Moral Thought*
   (3rd edition) (Routledge, 2003)
Simon Blackburn, *Being Good: An Introduction to Ethics* (OUP, 2001)
Simon Blackburn, *Ruling Passions* (Clarendon Press, 1998)
Colin Brown, *Crash Course on Christian Ethics* (Hodder & Stoughton,
   1998)
Steven M Cahn (ed.), *Classics of Western Philosophy* (4th edition)
   (Hackett Publishing Inc., 1995)
T L Carson and P K Moser (eds.), *Morality and the Good Life* (OUP
   USA, 1997)
Roger Crisp and Michael Slote (eds.), *Virtue Ethics* (OUP, 1997)
Jonathan Glover (ed.), *Utilitarianism and its Critics* (Macmillan USA,
   1990)
Bernard Haring, *Medical Ethics* (St Paul's Publications, 1972)
Jean Holm and John Bowker (eds.), *Making Moral Decisions*
   (Continuum International Publishing Group, 1994)
Ted Honderich, *How Free are You?* (OUP, 2002)
Alasdair MacIntyre, *A Short History of Ethics* (2nd edition)
   (Routledge, 2002)

Alasdair MacIntyre, *After Virtue* (Duckworth, 1982)
John L Mackie, *Ethics: Inventing Right and Wrong* (Penguin, 1977)
Anne Maclean, *The Elimination of Morality* (Routledge, 1993)
J Macquarrie and J Childs (eds.), *A New Dictionary of Christian Ethics* (SCM Press, 1986)
Bryan Magee, *Men of Ideas* (Oxford Paperbacks, 1982)
Iris Murdoch, *Metaphysics as a Guide to Morals* (Penguin, 1994)
Iris Murdoch, *The Sovereignty of Good* (Routledge Classics, 2001)
L P Pojman, *Ethics: Discovering Right and Wrong* (Wadsworth, 2001)
James Rachels, *The Elements of Moral Philosophy* (2nd edition) (McGraw-Hill, 1995)
Peter Singer(ed.), *A Companion to Ethics* (Blackwell, 1991)
Peter Singer, *How Are We To Live?: Ethics in an Age of Self-interest* (Mandarin, 1995)
J J C Smart and Bernard Williams, *Utilitarianism: For and Against* (CUP, 1973)
James P Sterba (ed.), *Ethics: the big questions* (Blackwell, 1998)
Avrum Stroll, *Did My Genes Make Me Do It?* (Oneworld, 2004)
Nigel Warburton, *Philosophy: The Classics* (2nd edition) (Routledge, 2001)
Mary Warnock, *An Intelligent Person's Guide to Ethics* (Duckworth, 1998)

Some classic works on ethics:
Saint Thomas Aquinas, *Summa Contra Gentiles* (University of Notre Dame Press, 1976)
Saint Thomas Aquinas, *Summa Theologica* (Christian Classics US, 2000)
Aristotle, *Nicomachean Ethics* (Dover Publications, 1998)
A J Ayer, *Language, Truth and Logic* (Dover Publications, 1952)
Jeremy Bentham, *An Introduction to the Principles of Morals and Legislation* (Prometheus Books, 1988)
Dietrich Bonhoeffer, *Ethics* (Pocket Books, 1995)
F H Bradley, *Ethical Studies* (Clarendon Press, 1962)
Epictetus (trans. George Long), *Enchiridion* (Dover Publications, 2004)
Joseph Fletcher, *Situation Ethics* (Westminster John Knox Press, 1966)
R M Hare, *Freedom and Reason* (Oxford Paperbacks, 1965)
R M Hare, *The Language of Morals* (Oxford Paperbacks, 1964)
Thomas Hobbes, *Leviathan* (Oxford World's Classics, 1998)
David Hume, *A Treatise of Human Nature* (Penguin, 1986)
Francis Hutcheson, *An Enquiry into the Original of Our Ideas of Beauty and Virtue* (G. Olms Verlag, 1990)
Immanuel Kant, *Critique of Practical Reason* (CUP, 1997)
Immanuel Kant, *Critique of Pure Reason* (CUP, 1999)
Immanuel Kant, *Groundwork of the Metaphysics of Morals* (CUP, 1998)

Søren Kierkegaard (trans. Alastair Hannay), *Either/Or* (Penguin Classics, 1992)

John Locke, *Two Treatises of Government* (CUP, 1988)

John Stuart Mill, *Utilitarianism* (OUP, 1998)

G E Moore, *Principia Ethica* (CUP, 1993)

Friedrich Nietzsche, *The Genealogy of Morals* (Dover Publications, 2003)

Friedrich Nietzsche, *Thus Spoke Zarathustra* (Penguin, 1978)

Friedrich Nietzsche, *Twilight of the Idols* (Penguin, 1990)

Friedrich Nietzsche, *Beyond Good and Evil* (Penguin, 1990)

Plato, *The Republic* (Penguin, 2003)

H A Prichard, *Moral Obligation* (OUP, 1963)

John Rawls, *A Theory of Justice* (revised edition) (OUP, 1999)

W David Ross, *The Foundations of Ethics* (OUP, 2000)

W David Ross, *The Right and the Good* (Clarendon Press, 2002)

Jean-Paul Sartre, *Existentialism and Human Emotions* (Citadel Press, 1984)

Henry Sidgwick, *Essays on Ethics and Method* (Clarendon Press, 2000)

C L Stevenson, *Ethics and Language* (Yale UP)

Paul Tillich, *Morality and Beyond* (Westminster John Knox Press, 2004)

Ludwig Wittgenstein, *Tractatus Logico-Philosophicus* (Routledge, 2001)

Websites:

The Stanford Encyclopedia of Philosophy
http://plato.stanford.edu/contents.html
This is an immense online resource. Just select Ethics from its range of subjects, and then go to particular theories, thinkers or topics.

The Internet Encyclopedia of Philosophy
www.utm.edu/research/iep/
This has a good range of relevant articles, and is particularly valuable for getting a historical perspective on the various ethical debates. Just select 'Ethics' from among the keywords.

Philosophy in Cyberspace
www-personal.monash.edu.au/~dey/phil/
This is a particularly useful site for the number of links it has with others. For those students who may be contemplating reading Philosophy at university, this has information about courses worldwide.

The Philosophers' Magazine
www.philosophersnet.com
'TPM Online' has an Ethics portal, through which to explore essays and notes on a huge range of topics.

Philosophy By Topic
http://users.ox.ac.uk/~worc0337/phil_topics.html
There is plenty of information here, both on individual topics and
thinkers, and also about university courses in philosophy worldwide.

Philosophy Pages
www.philosophypages.com/index.htm
There is loads of information on here – some parts more usable than
others.

There are many other sites, some offering information on a
particular ethical issue, or theory. For example, for straightforward
information from a site promoting modern utilitarianism, try:
www.utilitarianism.com

For anyone wanting to check details of other books on philosophy
and ethics by the same author, to ask anything about or comment
on this book, or to see additional material particularly suitable for
AS and A2 level students and their teachers in the United
Kingdom, log on to:

www.mel-thompson.co.uk

Index

Text Acknowledgements

Cambridge University Press, extract from *Principa Ethica* by G E Moore (1993), extracts from *Critique of Practical Reason* by Immanuel Kant (1997), extract from *Groundwork of the Metaphysics of Morals* by Immanuel Kant (1998); Citadel Press, extracts from *Existentialism and Human Emotions* by Jean-Paul Sartre (1984); Clarendon Press, extract from *Essays on Ethics and Method* by Henry Sidgwick (2000); Continuum International Publishing Group, extract from *The Christian Faith* by Friedrich Schleiermacher (1999); Dover Publications, extracts from *Nicomachean Ethics* by Aristotle (1998), extracts from *The Genealogy of Morals* by Friedrich Nietzsche (2003); Duckworth, extract from *After Virtue* by Alasdair MacIntyre (1982); George Bell and Sons, extract from *Fifteen Sermons* by Bishop Joseph Butler (1969); G Olms Verlag, extract from *An Enquiry into the Original of our Ideas of Beauty and Virtue* by Francis Hutcheson (1990); Hackett Publishing Inc., extract from *Classics of Western Philosophy, 4th edition: Encheiridion, Notes 8 & 14* ed. Steven M Cahn (1995), extract from *Twilight of the Idols* by Friedrich Nietzsche (1997); Methuen & Co, extract from *An Introduction to the Principles of Morals and Legislation* by Jeremy Bentham (1982); Oxford University Press, extracts from *Leviathan* by Thomas Hobbes (Oxford World's Classics, 1998), by permission of Oxford University Press, extract from *Utilitarianism* by John Stuart Mill (1998); Oxford Paperbacks, extract from *Men of Ideas* by Bryan Magee (1982); Penguin, extracts from *A Treatise of Human Nature* by David Hume (1986), extract from *Thus Spoke Zarathustra* by Friedrich Nietzsche (1978), extract from *Either/Or* by Søren Kierkegaard (trans. Alastair Hannay, 1992); Routledge, extract from *The Elimination of Morality* by Anne Maclean (1993), extracts from *The Sovereignty of Good* by Iris Murdoch (2001); SCM Press, extract from *A New Dictionary of Christian Ethics* eds. J Macquarrie and J Childs (1986); St Paul Publications, extract from *Medical Ethics* by Bernard Haring (1972); University of Notre Dame Press, extract from *Summa contra Gentiles* by Thomas Aquinas (trans. A C Pegis, 1976).